TREES

of the
Northern United States
and Canada

TREES

of the
Northern United States
and Canada

F. H. Montgomery

Formerly Head of the Department of Botany
University of Guelph

Frederick Warne & Co. Inc., New York

581.5
M

Colour plate 10 photograph by Monroe Landon
Cover photograph by Brant Cowie

Library of Congress Catalog No. 75-131362
ISBN 0-7700-0324-9

Printed and Bound in Canada by
John Deyell Ltd.

11/4/71 EBC 4.95(4.46)

CONTENTS

LIST OF FIGURES*

* Figures are approximately one-third natural size.

LIST OF COLOUR PLATES

Preface

In the great overall plan of nature, how fortunate it was that trees were included. In fact, they were a basic necessity in the plan if animal life was to exist. Directly, they provide food and shelter for the animals of the forest and much of the oxygen for all living things. Indirectly, they provide fertility for the soil, conserve our water supplies and supply man with lumber for his buildings, pulp for his newspapers and beauty for his soul.

Many are satisfied merely to be in a woods or forest and feel the grandeur of nature and their human insignificance in comparison with the giants of the forest. Some are happy only to hear the melody of bird songs issuing from the trees, or the low, soft sough of the wind through the boughs far above their heads.

Others, however, get a challenge to know the names of the trees that they see and enjoy, that the birds and animals are inhabiting and that supply so many of their needs. And then there are those whose hobby or business it is to know the trees. It is for these that this book is written.

Although it is primarily a book on trees, some shrubs are of necessity included. First, because it is often difficult to distinguish between a tree and a shrub; there is no clear cut line of demarcation. Second, under optimum growing conditions some species may be tree-like, while under poor conditions they may be shrubby. A third consideration is that in some genera there are both trees and shrubs. Where this occurs both shrubby and tree-like species are included for the sake of completeness.

The scientific names of the trees of the east are for the most part those used in *Manual of Vascular Plants of Northeastern United States and Adjacent Canada* by Gleason and Cronquist.* For those of the west, *Vascular Plants of the Pacific Northwest* by Hitchcock *et al* has been the source.

Common names vary from place to place and often several names are popular. The common names given in the manuals have been used here but those given in *Standardized Plant Names* are also in-

*Detailed descriptions of books mentioned in the text will be found in the bibliography.

cluded and in the text are the last common name listed for a species.

The keys are primarily based on mature leaf characteristics, but when fruit is available on the ground, or present or developing on the trees during the summer or autumn, they have been used as secondary characteristics. However, other features are helpful in identification and many of these have been included in the detailed descriptions. Barks and buds have been sparingly used since word descriptions are often inadequate to give a mental picture of them. They should, however, be carefully noted by the observer along with the other identifying features.

Two keys are given. The first leads to the genera. The second key is much more detailed and takes one to the species and a more complete description. As in most keys, there are two choices in each section, and one continues to select one of the alternatives until he reaches a description that fits the specimen that he is identifying. The keys are all illustrated and one can follow through them by observing illustrations alone. A key figure appearing on the right hand side of the page is repeated further along in the key on the left hand side of the page; a page number is also given to facilitate the search for it. One proceeds, then, from a right hand page figure to a similar figure on the left hand side of the page for the next step of his analysis.

After the keys there is a summary of leaf and fruit characters which can also be useful for identification. For example, one may have a tree with alternate leaves, simple teeth, and a red, stone fruit. By noting the trees in these categories and referring to the main text, it is possible to make a tentative identification.

Some species will appear two or three times in the keys. This is because their characteristics are not clear cut and can be interpreted in one or more ways.

My sincere thanks are extended to Mrs. David Ratz who prepared all the figures for the book. They have been drawn from specimens collected by the author or from his Kodachrome slides. Specimens of all but three species have been placed in the herbarium of the University of Waterloo, Waterloo, Ont.

I also wish to express my appreciation to field men of the Provincial or State Forestry Departments, or their equivalents, who assisted me in locating some of the less common trees. The help of my good friends Mr. Monroe Landon and Mr. Bert Miller has been invaluable in locating some almost extinct species in southern Ontario. Mr. H. E. Class very kindly read the manuscript and made many helpful suggestions. To all who have in any way contributed to the preparation of this book, my sincere thanks.

Key to the Tree Genera
Included in this Book

1. Leaves linear, needle-, scale-, or awl-like. The Evergreens or Gymnosperms. *Go to* 2.
1. Leaves not linear, needle-, scale-, or awl-like. The broad-leaved trees. *Go to* 11.

2. Leaves scale- or awl-like and arranged in opposite pairs or whorls of three; cones dry or somewhat fleshy and with a central stony seed; cones scales opposite or in whorls. The Cedars and Junipers. *Go to* 3.
2. Leaves linear or needle-like and arranged in spirals, fascicles or clusters. *Go to* 5.

3. Cone scales fused and fleshy enclosing a stony seed; leaves opposite or in whorls of three; branchlets rounded or 4-angled. The Junipers. *Juniperus* spp. *Go to page* 25.
3. Cone scales distinct and woody; branchlets flattened. The Cedars. *Go to* 4.

4. Cones globose, scales peltate, apically thickened and with a sharp, dorsal prickle. *Chamaecyparis* spp. *Go to page* 23.
4. Cones oval, scales thin and overlapping and without a sharp dorsal prickle. The Cedars. *Thuja* spp. *Go to page* 23.

5. Leaves clustered on short twigs or spurs and deciduous, therefore, only one season's growth of needles evident. The Larches or Tamaracks. *Larix* spp. *Go to page* 26.
5. Leaves not clustered on short twigs or spurs and not deciduous. *Go to* 6.

6. Leaves in fascicles of 2-5. The Pines. *Pinus* spp. *Go to page* 35.
6. Leaves single and spirally arranged on the branches or twigs, often twisted at their bases and appearing to be 2-ranked. *Go to* 7.

7. Branchlets roughened by the persistent bases of the leaves, bases decurrent on the twigs or branchlets. *Go to* 8.
7. Branchlets not roughened by the bases of the leaves, leaves sessile, scars flush with the branchlets or slightly raised and decurrent. *Go to* 10.

8. Leaves green on both surfaces and without white stomatal lines

on the lower surface; fruit red and fleshy, hollow at the apex and with a central stony seed. Yew. *Taxus* spp. *Go to page 29.*

8. Leaves with white stomatal lines on one or more surfaces; fruit woody cones. *Go to* 9.

9. Leaves sessile, sharp-pointed and most frequently 4-angled in cross section. The Spruces. *Picea* spp. *Go to page 29.*

9. Leaf bases contracted making the leaf appear short-stalked, leaves flat, apex not sharp-pointed. The Hemlocks. *Tsuga* spp. *Go to page 31.*

10. Cones stalked and drooping or pendant, scales persistent and subtended by a 3-pronged bract with the central prong the longest; leaves short-stalked, scars oval and slightly raised. Douglas Fir. *Pseudotsuga* spp. *Go to page 33.*

10. Cones sessile and erect, scales deciduous and the axis persistent on the branches; leaves sessile, scars circular and not raised. The Firs or Balsams. *Abies* spp. *Go to page 33.*

THE BROAD-LEAVED TREES

11. Leaves opposite on the twigs, or the twigs opposite on the branches. *Go to* 12.

11. Leaves alternate on the twigs, or the twigs alternate on the branches. *Go to* 19.

LEAVES OPPOSITE

12. Leaves simple. *Go to* 13.
12. Leaves compound. *Go to* 17.

13. Leaf margins lobed or sharply toothed, blades palmately veined and usually palmately lobed. The Maples. *Acer* spp. *Go to page 45.*

13. Leaf margins entire or with very low, rounded teeth; blades pinnately veined. *Go to* 14.

14. Leaf margins entire. *Go to* 15.
14. Leaf margins with small, low, rounded teeth. *Go to* 16.

15. Flowers and fruits in a terminal, stalked, branching inflorescence; fruits blue to black when mature and with a large, flat stone. *Viburnum* spp. *Go to page 42.*

15. True flowers in a cluster subtended by 4-6 large, white bracts; mature fruits clustered, red and with a central pit or stone. The Dogwoods. *Cornus* spp. *Go to page 42.*

13

16. Flowers and fruits from the axils of the leaves; twigs more or less 4-angled and the angles corky ridged; fruits 4-angled, purplish or pink when mature and splitting when ripe exposing the 4, red, pulp-covered seeds. *Euonymus* spp. *Go to page 43.*

16. Flowers terminal on the branches; inflorescence or fruiting clusters branching; fruits blue to black and with large, flat stones. *Viburnum* spp. *Go to page 43.*

17. Leaves usually with 3-5 leaflets, leaflets coarsely lobed or toothed; flowers and fruits developing on the current season's growth; fruits in pairs each one with a divergent wing; trees dioecious, with staminate flowers on different trees than the pistillate. Manitoba Maple. *Acer* spp. *Go to page 51.*

17. Leaves usually with 5-11 leaflets. *Go to* 18.

18. Flowers and fruits produced on the current season's growth and in large, branching, terminal inflorescences; fruits berry-like; small trees or shrubs. The Elderberries. *Sambucus* spp. *Go to page 51.*

18. Flowers and fruits in drooping panicles and axillary from buds on the previous year's growth; fruit dry, single and winged; trees dioecious. The Ashes. *Fraxinus* spp. *Go to page 53.*

LEAVES ALTERNATE

19. Leaves simple. *Go to* 20.
19. Leaves compound. *Go to* 58.

LEAVES ALTERNATE AND SIMPLE

20. Leaf margins lobed. *Go to* 21.
20. Leaf margins entire, toothed or wavy (sinuate). *Go to* 29.

21. Leaves more or less palmately lobed and at least the lowest veins going to the leaf lobes. *Go to* 22.

21. Leaves with the margins more or less pinnately lobed and all of the veins pinnate. *Go to* 27.

22. Leaves somewhat resembling Maple leaves, margins coarsely toothed, base of the petioles hollow or concave and covering the bud; outer bark scaling off; fruit a long-stalked, spherical cluster of hairy nutlets. Sycamore. *Platanus* spp. *Go to page 57.*

22. Leaves not resembling Maple leaves but with 2-4 lobes variously arranged. *Go to* 23.

23. Leaf lobes and margins sharply single- or double-toothed. *Go to 24.*

23. Leaf lobes and margins not toothed. *Go to 26.*

24. Fruit an oblong cluster of fleshy fruits (multiple) looking somewhat like a raspberry; leaves with 2 or more rounded lobes or simple, under surface pubescent. Mulberry. *Morus* spp. *Go to page 57.*

24. Fruits resembling miniature apples; small trees or shrubs. *Go to 25.*

25. Small trees or shrubs usually with slender or stout thorns; fruits red or purplish, 3/8 inch or more in diameter and with 1-5 hard nutlets. The hawthorns. *Crataegus* spp. *Go to page 59.*

25. Small trees or shrubs with short, slender, rough, thorn-like branchlets which may bear leaves, flowers or fruit, or, without thorny branchlets; fruits apple-like in cross section. The Crab Apples. *Pyrus* spp. *Go to page 59.*

26. Leaves 4-lobed with a broad, truncate apex with or without a shallow sinus, each lobe rather pointed, base of the petiole covering the bud; fruit a cone of winged fruits (samaras). Tulip Tree. *Liriodendron* spp. *Go to page 60.*

26. Leaves with 2 or 3 lobes or often simple, blades under magnification with translucent dots, pubescent on the lower surface, aromatic when bruised; fruit a blue stone fruit on a red, club-shaped stalk; branchlets smooth and green. Sassafras. *Sassafras* spp. *Go to page 60.*

27. Fruits acorns; lobes of the leaves acute and terminating with bristles, or the lobes rounded and entire, in some species the lobes become almost like large teeth; The Oaks. *Quercus* spp. *Go to page 60.*

27. Fruits like miniature apples; lobes of the leaves single- or double-toothed but without bristles. *Go to 28.*

28. Small trees or shrubs usually with slender or stout thorns; fruit red or purplish, 3/8 inch or more in diameter and with 1-5 nutlets. The Hawthorns. *Crataegus* spp. *Go to page 70.*

28. Small trees or shrubs with short, slender, rough, thorn-like branchlets which may bear leaves, flowers or fruit, or, without thorny branchlets; fruits apple-like in cross section. The Crab Apples. *Pyrus* spp. *Go to page 70.*

29. Margins of the leaves entire or some of the leaves on the same tree with lobes or enlarged teeth. *Go to* 30.

29. Margins of the leaves wavy (sinuate or undulate) or toothed. *Go to* 39.

30. Some of the leaves on the tree simple and others distinctly lobed or with obvious, enlarged teeth. *Go to* 31.

30. None of the leaves on the tree lobed. *Go to* 32.

31. Leaves simple or with 2 or 3 lobes, blades under magnification with translucent dots, pubescent on the lower surface, aromatic when bruised; fruit a blue stone fruit on a red, club-shaped stalk; branchlets smooth and green. Sassafras. *Sassafras* spp. *Go to page 71.*

31. Some of the leaves with entire margins and others with distant, pointed projections or lobes near the apex; leaves tending to be clustered at the ends of short branches; flowers and fruit axillary; fruit a dark, blue, stone fruit. Sour Gum. *Nyssa* spp. *Go to page 71.*

32. Fruits large and fleshy; leaves up to 12 inches long. *Go to* 33.

32. Fruits not large, consisting of bean-like pods, or berry-like, or arranged in catkins; leaves less than 6 inches long. *Go to* 34.

33. Leaves broadest near the apex and tapering to the base, short-stalked, rank-smelling when bruised; flowers purple or maroon and appearing along the branches before the leaves; fruit large and fleshy and containing seeds about 1 inch long. Pawpaw. *Asimina* spp. *Go to page 72.*

33. Leaves oval to elliptical, softly pubescent on the under surface; fruit a fleshy cone, reddish, oblique and curved. Cucumber Tree. *Magnolia* spp. *Go to page 72.*

34. Small trees; leaves rounded, heart-shaped at the base, slightly pubescent on the lower surface; fruit a bean-like pod. Redbud. *Cercis* spp. *Go to page 74.*

34. Leaves oval, oblong or elliptical; fruit not bean-like pods but berry-like or arranged in catkins. *Go to* 35.

35. Fruit capsules arranged in catkins and absent during the summer and fall; buds appressed to the twigs and with only one bud scale; trees or shrubs of moist habitats. The Willows. *Salix* spp. *Go to page 77.*

35. Fruits berry-like and usually present during the summer and early fall. *Go to* 36.

36. Leaves persistent, oval or oblong, thick and leathery, margins revolute, sometimes slightly toothed, surface dark green and shiny above, pale and reticulate (veiny) below; outer bark reddish and peeling off, inner bark bright reddish or orange colour. Arbutus. *Arbutus* spp. *Go to page 74.*
36. Leaves deciduous and not leathery. *Go to* 37.

37. Leaf veins extending to the leaf margins; leaves 2-7 inches long, broadly elliptical to oblong with a rounded apex with a very small apical point; margins obscurely toothed, under surface velvety pubescent. Cascara. *Rhamnus* spp. *Go to page 75.*
37. Leaf veins branching before reaching the leaf margins. *Go to* 38.

38. Flowers and fruits produced on a stalk arising in the axils of the leaves; leaves oval or broadest above the middle (obovate) and often slightly lobed or coarsely toothed near the apex; leaves tending to be clustered at the ends of short twigs. Sour Gum. *Nyssa* spp. *Go to page 75.*
38. Flowers and fruits in flat-topped, branching clusters (cymes) at the ends of the branches, fruits blue and on short, red stalks; leaves clustered at the ends of the branches. Dogwood species. *Cornus* spp. *Go to page 75.*

39. Margins of the leaves wavy, undulate or sinuate, with or without teeth, sometimes as in Oaks, the undulations may become almost large teeth. *Go to* 40.
39. Margins of the leaves distinctly toothed. *Go to* 42.

40. Base of the leaf asymmetrical, under surface slightly pubescent; terminal buds stalked, pubescent and without bud scales; flowers and fruits in the axils of the leaves, flowers yellow and appearing in the fall of one year and the fruits maturing in the following fall. Witch Hazel. *Hamamelis* spp. *Go to page 79.*
40. Base of the leaf symmetrical. *Go to* 41.

41. Fruits acorns; leaves tapering to the base; undulations or small lobes often resembling large teeth, secondary teeth or bristles absent. Some Oaks. *Quercus* spp. *Go to page 79.*
41. Fruits small, woody cones; leaves rounded at the bases, undulations or lobes toothed. The Alders. *Alnus* spp. *Go to page 81.*

42. Leaves asymmetrical at the base, margins single- or double-toothed or serrate. *Go to* 43.
42. Leaves symmetrical at the base, margins single- or double-toothed or serrate. *Go to* 45.

43. Leaves rather rounded, about as broad as long, heart-shaped at the base; flowers and fruits in branching, axillary clusters, peduncles with a bract or wing; fruit nut-like and pubescent. Basswood. *Tilia* spp. *Go to page 83*.

43. Leaves more or less oval or ovate, longer than broad. *Go to* 44.

44. Leaves broadest below the middle and tapering gradually to the slender apex, asymmetrical at the base, teeth simple, basal veins palmate; flowers and fruits arising from the axils of the leaves; fruit a cherry-like stone fruit. Hackberry. *Celtis* spp. *Go to page 83*.

44. Leaves broadest near the middle; veining pinnate and most of the veins not dividing at the margins; fruits thin, rounded samaras. The Elms. *Ulmus* spp. *Go to page 84*.

45. Nearly all the main veins of the leaf readily traceable to the leaf margins. *Go to* 46.

45. Nearly all of the veins of the leaf branching before reaching the leaf margins. *Go to 53*.

46. Teeth on the margins of the leaves simple but often irregular. *Go to* 47.

46. Teeth on the margins of the leaves double, or with large teeth or lobes followed by one or more smaller teeth. *Go to* 51.

47. Large trees; fruits spiny or bur-like nuts. *Go to* 48.

47. Trees or shrubs; fruits not bur-like or spiny, but berry-like, or arranged in catkins. *Go to* 49.

48. Teeth of the leaf margins short and straight; fruit small and bur-like containing 2, triangular or pyramidal nuts; bark smooth and gray. Beech. *Fagus* spp. *Go to page 86*.

48. Teeth of the leaf margins long and curving toward the leaf apex, apex long-pointed; fruit a globular, spiny bur about 2 inches in diameter. Chestnut. *Castanea* spp. *Go to page 86*.

49. Fruits berry-like, purple or black, leaves broadly elliptical to oblong with a rounded apex and a very small apical tip, margins obscurely toothed, under surface pubescent. Cascara. *Rhamnus* spp. *Go to page 88*.

49. Fruits arranged in catkins. *Go to* 50.

50. Shrubs; fruits in compact catkins, scales small; twigs often glandular. Birches. *Betula* spp. *Go to page 88*.

50. Small or large trees; flowers and fruits in open or loose catkins with bladder-like or wing-like bracts. Ironwood. *Ostrya* spp., or Blue Beech. *Carpinus* spp. *Go to page 89*.

51. Trees or shrubs of rather moist habitats; fruits in catkins and forming woody, persistent cones, cone bracts 3-5 lobed. The Alders. *Alnus* spp. *Go to page 91.*

51. Trees or shrubs of varying habitats; catkins not forming woody cones; bracts deciduous. *Go to 52.*

52. Trees or shrubs with compact catkins, bracts small, thin, entire or 3-lobed and deciduous. The Birches. *Betula* spp. *Go to page 92.*

52. Small or large trees; flowers and fruits in open or loose catkins with bladder-like or wing-like bracts. Ironwood. *Ostrya* spp., or Blue Beech. *Carpinus* spp. *Go to page 95.*

53. Fruits red and berry-like, somewhat resembling a raspberry; leaves simple or with 2 or more lobes, margins sharply and irregularly toothed, under surface pubescent. Mulberry. *Morus* spp. *Go to page 96.*

53. Fruits not berry-like. *Go to 54.*

54. Fruits arranged in catkins, but the capsules mature early in the spring and are usually absent when the leaves are mature. Poplars and Willows. In the absence of fruits, poplars may be recognized by the presence of a smooth, greenish or grayish bark usually occurring on some part of the tree, the buds have several bud scales. Willows inhabit moist habitats, the buds are appressed to the twigs and have only one bud scale. Poplar. *Populus* spp. and Willows. *Salix* spp. *Go to page 102.*

54. Fruits resembling miniature apples, or cherry- or plum-like. *Go to 55.*

55. Fruits cherry- or plum-like; when plum-like, the branches with short almost thorn-like branchlets. The Plums and Cherries. *Prunus* spp. *Go to page 98.*

55. Fruits small and apple-like. *Go to 56.*

56. Trees or shrubs without thorns and very variable in characteristics; flowers and fruits in racemes, fruits red to purplish. Juneberry, Service-berry, Shad-bush. *Amelanchier* spp. *Go to page 97.*

56. Small trees or shrubs with thorns or thorn-like branches. *Go to 57.*

57. Trees or shrubs with slender or stout, true thorns; fruits red or purplish and with 1-5 stony nutlets. The Hawthorns. *Crataegus* spp. *Go to page 97.*

57. Small trees or shrubs with short, slender, rough, thorn-like branchlets which may bear leaves, flowers and fruit, or, without thorny branchlets; fruits apple-like in cross section. Wild Crab Apple, *Pyrus* spp. *Go to page 97.*

LEAVES ALTERNATE AND COMPOUND

58. Leaves trifoliate and with translucent dots; fruit about 1/2-1 inch in diameter and broadly winged. Hop Tree. *Ptelea* spp. *Go to page 109.*
58. Leaves not trifoliate. *Go to 59.*
59. Leaves simple pinnate or bipinnate without a terminal leaflet (even pinnate). *Go to 60.*
59. Leaves simple pinnate or bipinnate but with a terminal leaflet present (odd pinnate). *Go to 62.*
60. Trees with the trunks and branches having stout, usually branched thorns; fruit a flat, curved or twisted, dark brown pod. Honey Locust. *Gleditsia* spp. *Go to page 110.*
60. Trees without thorns. *Go to 61.*
61. Leaves large with several (5-9) branches (leaflets) each pinnately divided; fruit a pod about 6 inches long and 2 inches broad, pod walls thick and leathery, seeds large. Kentucky Coffee Tree. *Gymnocladus* spp. *Go to page 110.*
61. Leaves simple pinnate, leaflets long taper-pointed; fruit a globose nut about 2 inches in diameter; pith of the twigs chambered or with cross partitions. Black Walnut. *Juglans* spp. *Go to page 110.*
62. Trees with the stipules modified to form thorns; fruits bean-like pods. Black Locust. *Robinia* spp. *Go to page 110.*
62. Trees without thorns and fruits not bean-like. *Go to 63.*
63. Flowers and fruits in flat-topped clusters, fruits small, red or orange and like miniature apples. Mountain Ashes. *Sorbus* spp. *Go to page 113.*
63. Fruit a nut, or berry-like and in racemes or dense clusters. *Go to 64.*
64. Small trees or shrubs; fruits berry-like in drooping panicles or compact, upright, cone-shaped clusters. The Sumacs. *Rhus* spp. *Go to page 114.*
64. Trees; fruits nuts with distinct husks. *Go to 65.*

65. Leaves with 11-23 leaflets; pith of the twigs chambered or with cross walls; husks of the nuts not splitting open when mature; fruits large, about 2 inches in diameter. Walnut and Butternut. *Juglans* spp. *Go to page 116.*
65. Leaves with 5-9 leaflets; pith of the twigs solid; husks of the nuts splitting open at maturity; leaves and fruits pleasantly aromatic. The Hickories. *Carya* spp. *Go to page 118.*

Key to the Tree Species

1. Leaves linear, needle-, scale- or awl-like. The Evergreens or Gymnosperms. *Go to page 22.*
2. Leaves not linear, needle-, scale- or awl-like. The broad-leaved trees. *Go to page 41.*

THE EVERGREENS OR GYMNOSPERMS

1. Leaves scale- or awl-like and arranged in opposite pairs or in whorls of three; cones dry or somewhat fleshy with central, stony seeds, cone scales opposite or in whorls. The Cedars and Junipers. *Go to page 22.*
2. Leaves linear or needle-like and arranged in spirals, fascicles or clusters. *Go to page 26.*

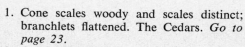

1. Cone scales woody and scales distinct; branchlets flattened. The Cedars. *Go to page 23.*
2. Cone scales fused and rather fleshy and with a central, stony seed; leaves opposite or in whorls of three; branchlets rounded or 4-angled. The Junipers. *Juniperus* spp. *Go to page 25.*

1. Cones globose, about 1/2 inch in diameter, scales 4 or 6, apically thickened, peltate, flattened and with a sharp, dorsal prickle; leaves opposite and appressed or the tips slightly spreading, bad smelling when crushed, often glandular on the back; trees tall, conical, branches horizontal or drooping, branchlets drooping; wood yellow. Pacific Coastal Region from Alaska south to California. Yellow Cedar, Yellow Cypress, Nootka Cypress. *Chamaecyparis nootkatensis* (D. Don) Spach. Fig. 1.

   White Cedar, *Chamaecyparis thyoides* extends northward along the Atlantic Coastal Plain to Maine.

2. Cones oval, scales thin and overlapping. *Go to the next key.*

1. Cones about 1/2 inch long and most frequently with 4 fertile scales, backs of the scales without a spine or point. Conical trees with a fibrous bark easily stripped from the trunk; branches erect to horizontal, branchlets flat, erect to horizontal or turned vertically. Moist or dry soils from Nova Scotia to Manitoba and north to James Bay; Maine to Minnesota, south to New York and Illinois. It has scattered distribution as far south as North Carolina and Tennessee. Arbor Vitae, Eastern White Cedar. *Thuja occidentalis* L. Fig. 2.

2. Cones about 1/2 inch long and most frequently with 6 fertile scales which have weak, spreading, dorsal spines. Large conical trees with a ridged, shredding bark; branches horizontal or descending and the branchlets flat, drooping or slightly upturned. Pacific Coastal Region from Alaska to California, east to the Selkirk Mountains and the Columbia River Basin. Western Red Cedar, Giant Arbor Vitae. *Thuja plicata* Donn. Fig. 3.

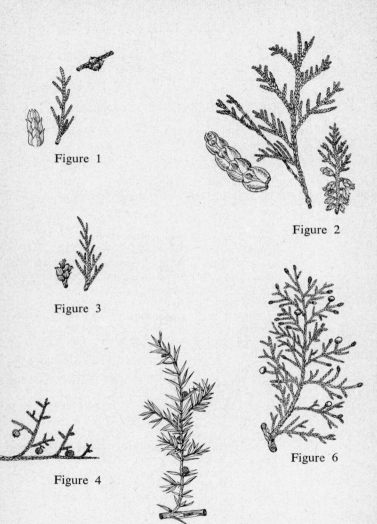

Figure 1

Figure 2

Figure 3

Figure 4

Figure 5

Figure 6

1. Prostrate shrubs with branches often rooting; leaves pointed; fruits drooping and on the under side of the branchlets. Newfoundland to British Columbia, north to Alaska, south through New England and west to Wyoming and Colorado. Creeping Juniper. *Juniperus horizontalis* Moench. Fig. 4.
2. Erect trees or shrubs. *Go to the next key*.

1. All of the leaves awl-like, sharp-pointed and in whorls of three; fruits blue or black and in the axils of the leaves, cone scales three. A bushy shrub across Canada and north to Alaska, south to Georgia, California and New Mexico. Common Juniper. *Juniperus communis* L. Fig. 5.

    At least four varieties of this species have been recognized.
2. None of the leaves awl-like, or only the leaves on younger twigs awl-like and in whorls of three, leaves of the older twigs scale-like and opposite; fruit terminal on the branchlets and erect or nodding. *Go to the next key*.

1. Cones forming stone fruits maturing the fall of their first year, therefore, all fruits similar in size and appearance. Eastern Red Cedar. *Juniperus virginiana* L. Fig. 6. The typical species is found from southern New England to Florida, Texas, Kentucky and Missouri. The var. *crebra* occurs in western Quebec and southern Ontario, north along the Georgian Bay and the Ottawa River, and south to Maine and New Hampshire.
2. Cones maturing in the fall of their second year, therefore, the branches have some well developed fruits and some quite immature fruits. Western Alberta and southern British Columbia east of the Cascades,

also reported on Vancouver Island, south through Washington, Oregon and the Rocky Mountains and Great Plain States as far as New Mexico. Rocky Mountain Juniper, Colorado Juniper. *Juniperus scopulorum* Sarg. Fig. 7.

The Western Juniper, *Juniperus occidentalis* Hook. is found chiefly in Oregon but is scattered in its distribution in Washington, Idaho, Nevada and California.

1. Leaves in a cluster on a short branch or spur and deciduous. Larch or Tamarack. *Larix* spp. *Go to page 26.*
2. Leaves neither clustered nor on a short spur and not deciduous. *Go to page 27.*

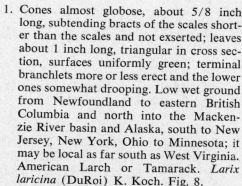

1. Cones almost globose, about 5/8 inch long, subtending bracts of the scales shorter than the scales and not exserted; leaves about 1 inch long, triangular in cross section, surfaces uniformly green; terminal branchlets more or less erect and the lower ones somewhat drooping. Low wet ground from Newfoundland to eastern British Columbia and north into the Mackenzie River basin and Alaska, south to New Jersey, New York, Ohio to Minnesota; it may be local as far south as West Virginia. American Larch or Tamarack. *Larix laricina* (DuRoi) K. Koch. Fig. 8.
2. Cones not globose, subtending bracts of the scales tapering to an awl-like tip longer than the scales and protruding from the cones; leaves about 1-1/2 inches long. *Go to the next key.*

1. Cone scales and twigs densely white-hairy at maturity; leaves 4-angled and with 2 resin ducts. A small tree found at high altitudes at or near the timber line in southwestern Alberta and British Columbia,

south to Washington, Idaho and Montana. Alpine Larch. *Larix lyallii* Pursh.

2. Cone scales with a slight pubescence, twigs not hairy at maturity or inconspicuously so; leaves more or less 3-angled in cross section, resin ducts not evident; tall trees with rough, scaly bark, terminal branchlets usually erect but the lower ones usually pendulous. Southeastern British Columbia and south into the adjacent States. Western Larch. *Larix occidentalis* Nutt. Fig. 9.

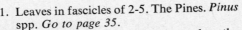

1. Leaves in fascicles of 2-5. The Pines. *Pinus* spp. *Go to page 35.*
2. Leaves single and spirally arranged on the branchlets or twigs, often twisted at their bases and appearing to be 2-ranked. *Go to the next key.*

1. Branchlets roughened by the persistent bases of the leaves, bases decurrent on the twigs or branches. *Go to page 27.*
2. Branchlets not roughened by the bases of the leaves, leaves sessile, scars flush with the branchlets or slightly raised and decurrent. *Go to page 33.*

1. Small trees or shrubs; leaves green on both surfaces and lacking white stomatal lines on the under surface, leaf bases contracted and appearing stalked; fruits red, fleshy and with a central, stony seed, fruit hollow at the apex and maturing in late summer or early fall. Yew. *Taxus* spp. *Go to page 29.*
2. Trees; leaves with white stomatal lines on one or more surfaces; fruits woody cones with spirally arranged scales. *Go to page 29.*

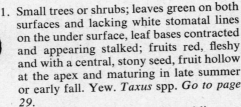

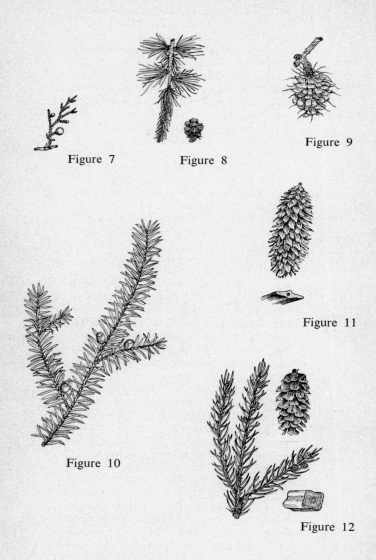

Figure 7

Figure 8

Figure 9

Figure 10

Figure 11

Figure 12

1. Bushy shrubs in woods from Newfoundland to Manitoba, south to Virginia; Kentucky and Iowa. Canada Yew. *Taxus canadensis* Marsh. Fig. 10.
2. Bushy shrubs or small, more or less contorted trees up to 25 feet high. Pacific Coastal Region from Alaska to California, east to south central British Columbia and Montana. Pacific Yew. *Taxus brevifolia* Nutt.

1. Leaves sessile, sharp-pointed and most frequently 4-angled in cross section. The Spruces. *Picea* spp. *Go to page 29.*
2. Leaf bases contracted making the leaf appear short-stalked, leaves flat, apex not sharp-pointed. The Hemlocks. *Tsuga* spp. *Go to page 31.*

1. Twigs glabrous. *Go to page 29.*
2. Twigs pubescent. *Go to page 30.*

1. Leaves thick but flattened and inconspicuously 4-angled, up to 1 1/2 inches long, stomata usually on only the upper surface, or also with 2 less conspicuous stomatal lines on the lower surface; cones 2 1/4-4 inches long, scales stiff, somewhat oblong in outline, apex truncate and erose or ragged; large trees with dark, scaly bark. Pacific Coastal Region from Alaska to California. Sitka Spruce. *Picea sitchensis* (Bong.) Carr. Fig. 11.

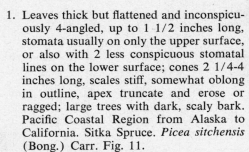

2. Leaves 4-sided with white stomatal lines on each surface, crowded toward the upper side of the branches by a twisting of the bases; cone 1 1/2-2 inches long, usually terminal on the branches, cylindrical, scales thin, flexible, entire, rounded at the apex; tip of the younger twigs glaucous; buds glabrous. Newfoundland to British Columbia and Alaska., south to Montana

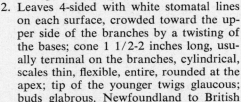

and east to northern Minnesota, Michigan, New York and Maine. White Spruce. *Picea glauca* (Moench.) Voss. Fig. 12.

1. Cones elliptical or cylindrical, 1 1/2-2 1/2 inches long, scales flexible, rounded or more or less tapering at the apex, margins wavy, ragged or erose; branches sloping upward at the top of the trees and becoming drooping near the base, branchlets often pendulous; stomata on all surfaces; new twigs green and not glaucous; bark brownish, thin and scaly. The Rocky Mountains of Western Alberta and British Columbia, south to New Mexico and Arizona. Also on the east slopes of the Coast Range of British Columbia and the Cascades from Washington to California. Engelmann Spruce. *Picea engelmannii* Parry ex Engelm. Fig. 13.

2. Cone scales stiff or rigid, rounded at the apex. *Go to the next key*.

1. Cones ovate to almost globose, 1/2-1 inch long and persistent on the branches for some years, scales with irregular, ragged or erose margins; leaves bluish-green with a whitish bloom. Bogs and marshes across Canada to Alaska, south to New York, Michigan, Wisconsin and Minnesota. Black Spruce. *Picea mariana* (Mill.) B.S.P. Fig. 14.
2. Cones 1-2 inches long, elliptical or conical in shape and deciduous, scales stiff, rounded at the apex, entire or slightly ragged or erose; leaves glossy green and without a whitish bloom. Rocky soils from Nova Scotia to eastern Ontario, Algonquin Park and vicinity, south to Maine and New York and scattered through the Appalachian Mountains to North Carolina and Tennessee. Red Spruce. *Picea rubens* Sarg. Fig. 15.

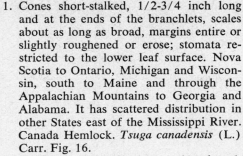

1. Cones short-stalked, 1/2-3/4 inch long and at the ends of the branchlets, scales about as long as broad, margins entire or slightly roughened or erose; stomata restricted to the lower leaf surface. Nova Scotia to Ontario, Michigan and Wisconsin, south to Maine and through the Appalachian Mountains to Georgia and Alabama. It has scattered distribution in other States east of the Mississippi River. Canada Hemlock. *Tsuga canadensis* (L.) Carr. Fig. 16.
2. Cones sessile, scales longer than broad; apical shoot of the trees drooping. Species of the western Mountains. *Go to the next key.*

1. Leaves somewhat 4-sided, standing out on all sides of the twigs, stomatal lines on both the upper and lower surfaces; cones 2-3 inches long, scales rounded and slightly ragged or erose on the margin; leader shoot of the trees erect on younger trees and only slightly drooping on the older trees. A tree of high altitudes in the Pacific Coastal Region from Alaska to California and in the Selkirk Mountains of British Columbia, south to Idaho and Montana. Mountain Hemlock. *Tsuga mertensiana* (Bong.) Carr.
2. Leaves appearing as if two-ranked, often inverted and showing the white stomatal lines of the under surface; cones oval, about 1 inch long; leader shoot of the trees drooping. Pacific Coastal Region from Alaska to northern California and in the Selkirk Mountains and Columbia River Basin of British Columbia, south to Idaho and Montana. *Tsuga heterophylla* (Raf.) Sarg. Fig. 17.

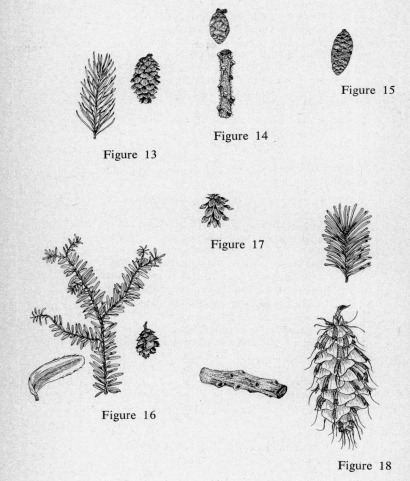

Figure 13

Figure 14

Figure 15

Figure 16

Figure 17

Figure 18

1. Cones stalked and drooping, scales persistent, hairy and subtended by a protruding 3-pronged bract with the central prong the longest; leaves short-stalked, rounded at the apex and irregularly divergent on the twig, bases leaving only a slightly raised, oval, hollow scar on the twigs; lower branches drooping and the branchlets pendant. Southern British Columbia and western Alberta, south to California and western Texas. Douglas Fir. *Pseudotsuga menziesii* (Mirabel) Franco. Fig. 18.

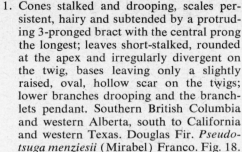

2. Cones near the tops of the trees, sessile and erect at the ends of the previous year's growth, scales deciduous and leaving the persistent, spike-like axis on the trees, (they can be seen easily near the tops of the trees with the aid of binoculars); leaves sessile and leaving a circular, depressed scar when they fall; branches most frequently in whorls of 4 or 5, spreading and fan-like. The Balsams or Firs. *Abies* spp. *Go to the next key.*

1. Leaves twisted at their bases and appearing as if 2-ranked. *Go to page 33.*
2. Leaves, at least some of them, not appearing 2-ranked, overlapping and often turned upward. *Go to page 34.*

1. Leaves 3/4-2 1/4 inches long, stomata on the lower surface only, tips of the leaves notched; cones 2-4 1/2 inches long, cylindrical, scales broader than long; conical trees with the branches drooping but the terminal branchlets turned upward; the leaf arrangement often makes it appear as if the longest leaves were at the middle of the season's growth. Southwestern British Columbia and Vancouver Island, south to California, and in the Columbia River basin of British Columbia, south to Idaho

and Montana. Giant or Grand Fir, Great
Silver Fir. *Abies grandis* (Dougl.) Lindl.
Fig. 19.

2. Leaves 3/4-1 1/4 inches long and not as
variable in length on the branchlets. *Go
to the next key.*

1. Cones 1 1/4-3 1/2 inches long, more or
less cylindrical, scales broader at the apex
than at the base and usually longer than
broad; stomata on the lower surface of the
leaves only, or a few at the tip of the
upper surface, apex of the leaves pointed
or only slightly notched; bark scaly. Newfoundland and Labrador to northern
Alberta, Minnesota, Wisconsin and Michigan, south to Maine, New York and
Pennsylvania. Occasional as far south as
Virginia and Iowa. Balsam Fir. *Abies bal-
samea* (L.) Mill. Fig. 20.

2. Cones 4-6 inches long, scales about as
broad as long; leaves of the upper surface
of the branchlets shorter than those of the
lower surface and appressed forward making a V arrangement, those of the lower
surface more or less turned upward, tips
notched or pointed on the cone-bearing
branches, upper surface deeply grooved,
stomata mostly on the lower surface or a
few at the tip of the upper surface; slender conical trees with grayish bark marked
by white patches; branches curving downward. Pacific Coastal Region from Alaska
to California. Lovely Fir, Amabilis Fir,
Cascade Fir. *Abies amabilis* (Dougl.)
Forbes. Fig. 21.

1. Cones 2-4 inches long; stomata on both
the upper and lower surfaces of the leaves,
leaves turned upward, apices not notched
or only slightly so; trees slender, conical,

spire-like; branches short and the lower branches bending downward. Alaska and Yukon south to Oregon, and in the Rocky Mountains to Arizona and New Mexico. Alpine Fir. Rocky Mountain Fir. *Abies lasiocarpa* (Hook.) Nutt. Fig. 22.

2. Cones 4-6 inches long. Cascade Fir, *Abies amabilis* could also be included in this key section. *For description see page 34.*

White Fir, *Abies concolor* is to be found in southern Oregon and Idaho, and Noble Fir, *A. procera* occurs in the Pacific Coastal Region of Oregon and Washington.

1. Leaves in fascicles of 5. *Go to page 35.*
2. Leaves in fascicles of 2 or 3. *Go to page 37.*

1. The only native eastern pine with 5 leaves; cones cylindrical, 3-10 inches long, long-stalked, slightly curved. Newfoundland to Manitoba, Minnesota, Wisconsin and Michigan, south through Maine, New York, Pennsylvania and the Appalachian Mountains to South Carolina and Georgia. White Pine. *Pinus strobus* L. Fig. 23.
2. Trees found in the western mountain region. *Go to the next key.*

1. Trees of medium to large size, conical or narrow-columnar in stands, branches horizontal to drooping; bark grayish and smooth when young but becoming broken into squarish plates with age; cones 8-10 inches long, short-stalked, scales thin, rounded at the apex; leaves 2-4 inches long, apex blunt. Pacific Coastal Region from British Columbia to California, and the Selkirk Mountains of British Columbia to Montana, Idaho and Washington. Western White Pine. *Pinus monticola* Dougl. ex D. Don. Fig. 24.

Figure 19

Figure 21

Figure 20

Figure 23

Figure 22

Figure 24

Figure 25

2. Trees of high altitudes, usually close to the timber line; small, often dwarfed, contorted trees. *Go to the next key.*

1. Cones 3-10 inches long, scales narrow, pointed and separating at maturity, cones dropping intact; seeds with narrow wings; leaves about 3 inches long, stiff and clustered at the ends of the branches; annual growth scars on the twigs very evident, branches flexible, bark grayish. At high elevations in western Alberta and eastern British Columbia, south through Montana and Idaho to California, Arizona and New Mexico. Limber Pine. *Pinus flexilis* James. Fig. 25.

2. Very similar to the previous species; cones oval or rounded, 1 1/2-3 inches long, scales remaining closed at maturity for some time, tips of the scales with a sharp, curved prickle, cones not falling intact; seeds wingless; leaves 1 1/2-2 1/2 inches long, rather rigid and clustered at the ends of the branches; twigs as in the previous species; bark with whitish scales. At high attitudes in southern British Columbia and southwestern Alberta, south to California, Montana, Idaho to Nevada. Whitebark Pine. *Pinus albicaulis* Engelm.

1. Leaves most frequently in clusters of 3. *Go to page 37.*
2. Leaves most frequently in clusters of 2. *Go to page 38.*

1. Small trees with rough scaly bark; cones egg-shaped (ovate) and persistent on the branches, scales with short, stiff, recurved prickles; leaves 1 1/2-5 1/2 inches long. Southwestern Quebec and in Ontario on the Canadian Shield outcrop between Gananoque and Brockville, south in the

New England States, New York and through the Appalachians to South Carolina and Georgia. Pitch Pine. *Pinus rigida* Mill. Fig. 26.

2. Tall, stout trees; cones deciduous, almost sessile near the ends of the branches or branchlets, 3-6 inches long, scales with strong, terminal prickles; leaves most frequently in 3's but occasionally in fascicles of 2, 4 or 5, leaves clustered near the ends of the branches; bark thick, brownish-red or cinnamon colour and forming scales that drop off. The most widespread 3-leaved pine in the western mountains. Southern interior of British Columbia, south through the mountain States to California, Arizona and New Mexico. Ponderosa Pine, Yellow Pine, Bull Pine. *Pinus ponderosa* Dougl. ex Loud. Fig. 27.

1. Cones not long persistent on the branches; cones oval or egg-shaped (ovate), 1 1/2-2 inches long and opening at maturity, almost terminal on the twigs, symmetrical in form, scales without prickles; leaves 3 1/2-6 1/2 inches long; bark reddish. Newfoundland and Nova Scotia to Manitoba, Minnesota, Wisconsin and Michigan, south through New England, New York and Pennsylvania, local elsewhere. Red Pine. *Pinus resinosa* Ait. Fig. 28.

2. Cones persistent for some years after the maturing of the seeds; leaves 3/4-3 inches long. *Go to the next key.*

1. Leaves 1 1/4-3 inches long; cones 1 1/4-2 inches long, somewhat egg-shaped and asymmetrical, scales with slender, curved prickles; trees tall, slender-conical or with rather straight sides when growing in stands, bark thin and scaly, tips of the branches turned upward. Alaska, Yukon

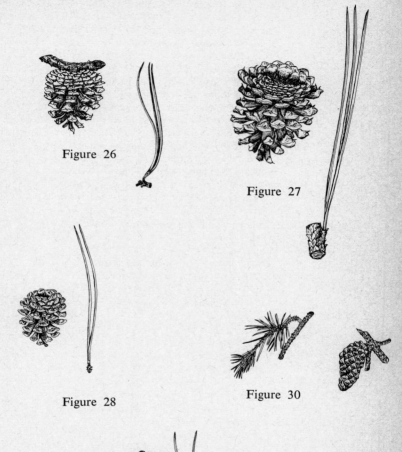

Figure 26

Figure 27

Figure 28

Figure 30

Figure 29

south through British Columbia and western Alberta to Colorado, Nevada and California. Local in the Cypress Hills. Lodgepole Pine *Pinus contorta*. Dougl. ex. Loud. Fig. 29.

The typical Lodgepole Pine is considered by some botanists to be *P. contorta* var. *latifolia* Engelm. ex S. Wats. On the Pacific Coast it is called the Shore Pine, *Pinus contorta* var. *contorta* and it may be recognized by its rather deformed symmetry, smaller cones and shorter leaves.

2. Leaves 3/4-1 1/2 inches long, twisted and widely divergent; cones lateral on the twigs, about 1 1/2-2 inches long, conical, asymmetrical at the base, curved and often appressed to the branches, scales with small, weak prickles which are easily removed. Nova Scotia northwest to the Mackenzie River Basin, south to Alberta, Saskatchewan, Manitoba, Minnesota, Wisconsin, and Michigan, less common in New England and New York. Jack Pine. *Pinus banksiana* Lamb. Fig. 30.

In addition to the above, some pines of the Southern States enter the northern States.

Shortleaf or Yellow Pine, *Pinus echinata*, is widely distributed in the Southern States and extends north to Montana and north east to southeastern New York. The leaves are in 2's or 3's and 3-5 inches long.

Table-mountain pine, *Pinus pungens*, is a pine of the Appalachian Mountains from Georgia north to Pennsylvania and New Jersey. Its most distinctive feature is the cone which has long, stout spines.

Pond Pine, *Pinus serotina* extends north on the Coastal Plain from Florida to Delaware The leaves are in 3's and 5 to 10 inches long. The cones are 2 3/4 inches or more long.

Loblolly Pine, *Pinus taeda* is also a pine of the southern States and reaches Delaware along the Coastal Plain. The leaves are in 3's, 5-10 inches long and the cones are less than 2 1/2 inches long.

Virginia or Scrub Pine, *Pinus virginiana* is a small tree of the dry soils of the foothills of the Appalachians and edge of the Coastal Plain from Alabama to southern New York. The leaves are in 2's and 1 1/2-3 inches long.

THE BROAD-LEAVED TREES

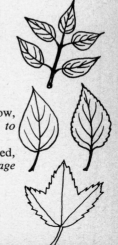

1. Leaves opposite on the twigs, or the twigs opposite on the branches. *Go to page 41.*
2. Leaves alternate on the twigs, or the twigs alternate on the branches. *Go to page 56.*

LEAVES OPPOSITE

1. Leaves simple. *Go to page 41.*
2. Leaves compound. *Go to page 51.*

LEAVES OPPOSITE AND SIMPLE

1. Leaf margins entire or with very low, rounded teeth, pinnately veined. *Go to page 42.*
2. Leaf margins lobed or sharply toothed, veining or lobing palmate. *Go to page 45.*

41

1. Leaf margins entire. *Go to page 42.*
2. Leaf margins with small, low, rounded teeth. *Go to page 43.*

1. Small trees or shrubs; flowers and fruits in a stalked, terminal, branching inflorescence; fruit when mature blue to black with a whitish bloom and a large, flat stone; winter buds with 2, yellowish scales; leaves ovate, or broader above the middle, abruptly pointed at the apex, margin slightly thickened. Newfoundland and Nova Scotia to Ontario, south to Maryland and Indiana, and through the Appalachian Mountains to Florida and Alabama. Wild Raisin, Withe-rod. *Viburnum cassinoides* L. Fig. 31.

2. True flowers in a central cluster subtended by 4-6 large, white bracts; mature fruits clustered, red and with a central pit or stone; leaves pinnately veined; small trees or shrubs. *Go to the next key.*

1. Small trees or shrubs of the Pacific Coastal Region; flower cluster surrounded by 4-6 bracts which are usually pointed at the apex; leaves oval, elliptical or somewhat oblong, rather abruptly pointed at the apex, pubescent on both surfaces, veins prominent; leaves tending to be clustered at the ends of the branches; fruits numerous and clustered. Pacific Coastal Region of British Columbia south to California. It is also reported locally inland. Western Dogwood, Pacific Dogwood. *Cornus nuttallii* (Aud.) T. & G. Fig. 32.

    The floral emblem of British Columbia.
2. Small trees or shrubs of southern Ontario; bracts subtending the flower clusters usually 4, broad and heart-shaped at the apex; leaves often clustered at the ends of the

branches, oval or elliptical, rather abruptly pointed at the apex, veins prominent, blades pubescent on both surfaces; branchlets greenish; fruits red, and few in a cluster. Southern Maine, west to southern Ontario and Michigan, south to Florida and Texas, north to Montana and Illinois. Flowering Dogwood. *Cornus florida* L. Fig. 33.

1. Flowers and fruits in branching clusters from the axils of the leaves; leaves finely or minutely pubescent on the under surface; twigs often more or less 4-angled and the angles with cork-like ridges; fruit 4-angled, purplish or pinkish when mature and splitting when ripe exposing the 4, red, pulp-covered seeds. Small trees or shrubs from New York to southern Ontario and Minnesota, south to Florida and Texas Burning Bush, Wahoo. *Euonymus atropurpureus* Jacq. Fig. 34.
2. Flowers and fruits terminal on the branches. *Go to the next key.*

1. Small trees or shrubs; flowers and fruits in a stalked, terminal, branching inflorescence; fruit when mature blue to black with a whitish bloom and a large, flat stone; winter buds with 2, yellowish scales; leaves ovate or obovate, abruptly pointed at the apex, margin slightly thickened. Newfoundland and Nova Scotia to Ontario, south to Maryland and Indiana, and through the Appalachian Mountains to Florida and Alabama. Wild Raisin, Withe-rod. *Viburnum cassinoides* L. Fig. 31.
2. Inflorescence or fruiting clusters not stalked, but much branched as in the previous species; fruit blue with a large, flat stone; teeth of the leaf margins calloustipped, petiole wing-margined, leaf apex

43

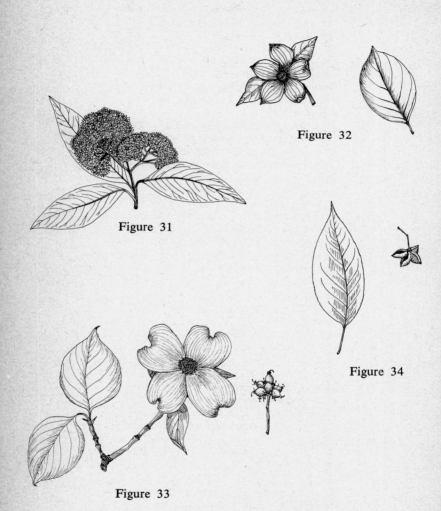

Figure 32

Figure 31

Figure 34

Figure 33

long-pointed; winter bud scales 2 and grayish. Western Quebec to Saskatchewan, and Maine south to Georgia and west to South Dakota and Colorado. Nannyberry. *Viburnum lentago* L. Fig. 35.

1. Leaves 7-9-lobed, the lobes sharply toothed, pubescent on the lower surface particularly in the axils of the lower veins, veins of the upper surface pubescent; wings of the fruit almost horizontal. Small trees or shrubs, often clumped and bushy. Most frequent in the Pacific Coastal Region from Alaska to California. Vine Maple. *Acer circinatum* Pursh. Fig. 36.
2. Leaves with 3-5 lobes. *Go to the next key*.

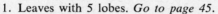

1. Leaves with 5 lobes. *Go to page 45*.
2. Leaves with 3 lobes. *Go to page 49*.

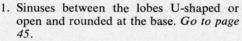

1. Sinuses between the lobes U-shaped or open and rounded at the base. *Go to page 45*.
2. Sinuses between the lobes V-shaped or deep and narrow or angled at the base. *Go to page 47*.

1. Under surface of the leaves without hairs; margins distinctly 5-lobed and irregularly toothed, sinuses open, blades flat. Nova Scotia to western Ontario and Minnesota, south to Georgia and Missouri. Sugar Maple. *Acer saccharum* Marsh. Fig. 37.
   The floral emblem of New Jersey.
2. Under surface of the leaves usually soft-pubescent; margins distinctly 3-lobed and with 2 additional indistinct basal lobes, margins with few teeth and usually drooping as if wilted. Southwestern Quebec to Minnesota, south to Vermont, New York to Tennessee and Missouri. Black Maple. *Acer nigrum*. Michx. f. Fig. 38.

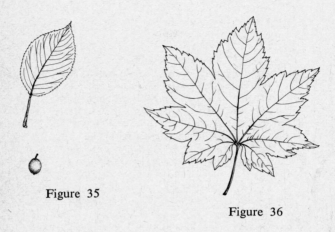

Figure 35

Figure 36

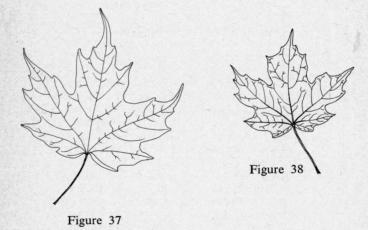

Figure 37

Figure 38

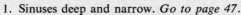

1. Sinuses deep and narrow. *Go to page 47.*
2. Sinuses comparatively shallow and open. *Go to page 47.*

1. Leaves 8-12 inches broad, slightly pubescent on both surfaces, margins not sharply toothed, petioles up to 12 inches long; fruits in drooping clusters or racemes and pubescent; large trees, bark smooth at first but becoming narrowly ridged. Pacific Coastal Region from British Columbia to California. Broad-leaved Maple, Oregon Maple. *Acer macrophyllum* Pursh. Fig. 39.

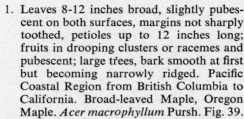

2. Leaves deeply 5-lobed, about 5 inches broad, petioles up to 5 inches long, under surface of the blades glabrous and silvery, margins irregularly and sharply toothed; fruits pubescent. New Brunswick to southern Ontario and Minnesota, south to Maine, Florida and Oklahoma. Silver Maple. *Acer saccharinum* L. Fig. 40.

1. Small trees or shrubs with reddish-brown bark and twigs; leaf margins sharply and doubly toothed, veins prominent, blade glabrous or slightly glandular pubescent. Southwestern Alberta, British Columbia and Alaska, south to California, New Mexico and Nebraska. Dwarf Maple, Rocky Mountain Maple. *Acer glabrum* Torr. Fig. 41.

    Two varieties of this species are recognized, the typical *A. glabrum* and the var. *douglasii.*
2. Trees with gray bark and reddish twigs; flowers reddish and appearing before the leaves; under surface of the leaves rather silvery, sinuses shallow, margins coarsely and often doubly toothed; fruit glabrous. Newfoundland and Nova Scotia to Ontario and Minnesota, south to Florida and Texas. Red Maple. *Acer rubrum* L. Fig. 42.

Figure 39

Figure 40

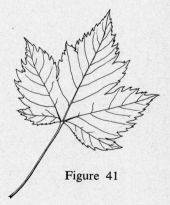

Figure 41

1. Leaves distinctly 3-lobed; flowers in racemes. *Go to page 49.*
2. Leaves with 3 distinct lobes and often with a pair of small indistinct basal lobes; flowers not in racemes. *Go to page 49.*

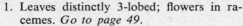

1. Flowers and fruits in erect racemes; leaf margins coarsely toothed, under surface of the leaves somewhat pubescent. Small trees or shrubs from Newfoundland to Saskatchewan, south to New England, Tennessee, and northwest to Iowa. Mountain Maple. *Acer spicatum* Lam. Fig. 43.
2. Flowers and fruits in drooping racemes; leaves finely toothed, tips of the lobes long-pointed; bark with dark or pale stripes. Small trees or shrubs from Nova Scotia to northern Ontario and Minnesota, south to Maine, North Carolina and Tennessee. Moosewood, Striped Maple. *Acer pensylvanicum* L. Fig. 44.

1. Small trees or shrubs with reddish-brown bark and twigs; leaf margins sharply and doubly toothed, veins prominent; blade glabrous or slightly glandular pubescent. Southwestern Alberta, British Columbia and Alaska, south to California, New Mexico and Nebraska. Dwarf Maple, Rocky Mountain Maple. *Acer glabrum* Torr. Fig. 41.

   Two varieties of this species are recognized, the typical *A. glabrum* and the var. *douglasii.*
2. Trees with gray bark and reddish twigs; flowers reddish and appearing before the leaves; under surface of the leaves rather silvery, sinuses shallow, margins coarsely and often doubly toothed; fruits glabrous. Newfoundland and Nova Scotia to Ontario and Minnesota, south to Florida and Texas. Red Maple. *Acer rubrum* L. Fig. 42.

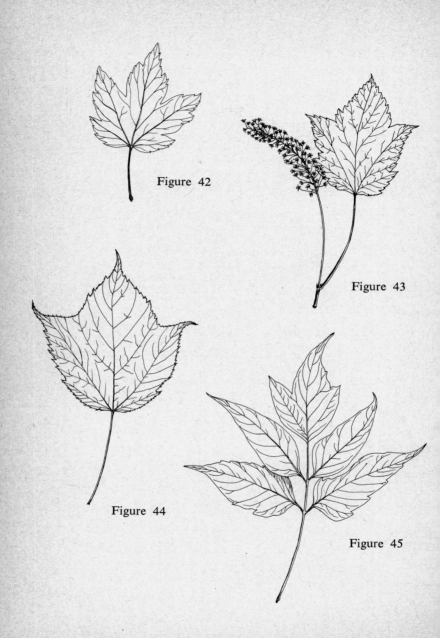

Figure 42

Figure 43

Figure 44

Figure 45

1. Leaves with usually 3-5 leaflets, occasionally 7, leaflets lobed or coarsely toothed; flowers and fruits developed on the current season's growth and male and female flowers on separate trees; ovary 2-lobed and when mature each lobe winged; twigs gray, often with a whitish bloom, very brittle. Native, cultivated or naturalized in most of the Canadian Provinces and the American States except those of the far west. Manitoba Maple, Box Elder. *Acer negundo* L. Fig. 45.

   Several varieties of this species have been described.

2. Leaves with 5-11 or more leaflets; margins of the leaflets entire, wavy or toothed. *Go to the next key.*

1. Flowers and fruits produced on the current season's growth; leaves usually with 5-9 leaflets; leaflet asymmetrical at the base, margins toothed and the teeth calloused; inflorescence large and flat-topped, very branching; berry-like fruit small, black or blue and covered with a heavy whitish bloom. Shrubs or small trees from southern British Columbia and Montana to California and New Mexico. Blueberry Elder. *Sambucus cerulea* Raf. (*S. glauca* Nutt.) Fig. 46.

A second species of Elderberry that may become tree-like under favourable conditions is *S. racemosa* var. *arborescens* (T. & G.) Gray. Fig. 47. It is a western species and is recognized by its rounded or convex inflorescence and red or black fruit with a whitish bloom.

The shrubby *S. racemosa* var. *pubens* (Michx.) Koen., (*S. pubens* Michx.) is a common species in eastern Canada and east-

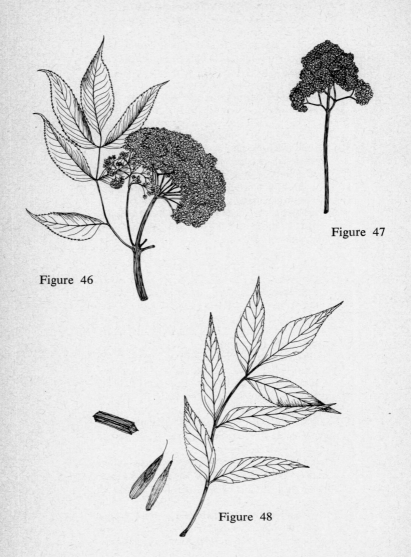

Figure 46

Figure 47

Figure 48

ern States and extends westward to British Columbia. It blooms in early spring and has a brownish pith and red fruit.

S. canadensis L., American Elder, is also a common shrub in the east and is found as far west as Manitoba and south to the southern States. It flowers later and has a white pith and blue or black fruit.

2. Flowers and fruits produced from buds on the previous year's growth; male and female flowers on separate trees; ovary 1-lobed and the fruit winged. *Go to next key*.

1. Branchlets or twigs 4-angled, angles more or less winged with cork-like ridges; leaflets short-stalked, margins toothed; fruits winged to the base; older bark somewhat scaly. Western New York, one or two stations in Ontario, west to Wisconsin and Kansas, south to Oklahoma and Alabama. Blue Ash. *Fraxinus quadrangulata* Michx. Fig. 48.

2. Branchlets not 4-angled. *Go to the next key*.

1. Leaflets 7-11, sessile except for the terminal leaflet, margins sharply serrate; fruits winged to the base. Newfoundland and Nova Scotia to Manitoba, south to West Virginia and Iowa. Black Ash *Fraxinus nigra* Marsh. Fig. 49.

2. Leaflets stalked. *Go to the next key*.

1. Stalks of the leaflets not winged; leaflets whitish on the under surface and glabrous, margins entire or with wavy or low teeth; fruit not winged to the base; bark finely and deeply grooved. Nova Scotia to Ontario, Wisconsin and Nebraska, south to Florida and Texas. White Ash. *Fraxinus americana* L. Fig. 50.

2. Stalks of the leaflets winged. *Go to the next key*.

Figure 49

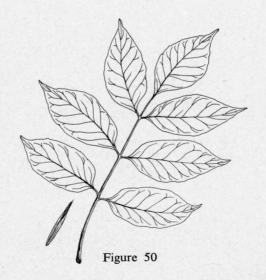

Figure 50

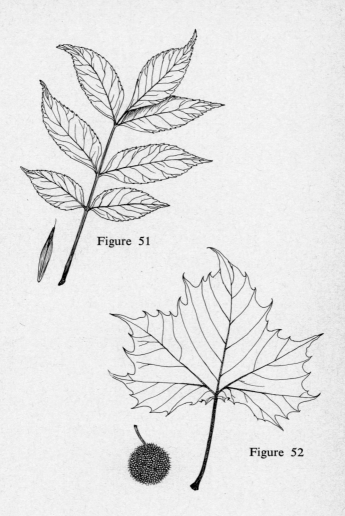

Figure 51

Figure 52

1. Twigs, leaf stalks and under surface of the leaflets densely soft pubescent; margins of the leaflets wavy or with low teeth. Southwestern Quebec, New England, New York, west to Manitoba and Minnesota. Red Ash. *Fraxinus pennsylvanica* Marsh.
2. Twigs, leaf stalks and under surface of the leaflets not pubescent, or pubescent only on the lower veins; margins of the leaflets more or less toothed. Quebec to Saskatchewan, south to New England, Florida and Texas. Green Ash. *Fraxinus pennsylvanica var. subintegerrima* (Vahl.) Fern. Fig. 51.

Ohio Buckeye, *Aesculus glabra* occurs from western Pennsylvania and southern Michigan to Iowa and south to Alabama and Texas. It does not occur in Canada except when planted. It is easily recognized by its opposite, palmately compound leaves of 5-7 leaflets, and the large, spiny, capsule-like fruit.

LEAVES ALTERNATE

1. Leaves simple. *Go to page 56.*
2. Leaves compound. *Go to page 109.*

LEAVES ALTERNATE AND SIMPLE

1. Leaf margins lobed. *Go to page 57.*
2. Leaf margins entire, wavy (undulate) or toothed. *Go to page 71.*

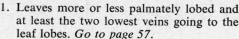

1. Leaves more or less palmately lobed and at least the two lowest veins going to the leaf lobes. *Go to page 57.*
2. Leaves with the margins more or less pinnately lobed and all the veins pinnate. *Go to page 60.*

1. Leaves somewhat resembling maple leaves, palmately lobed and veined, base truncate or only slightly heart-shaped, margins coarsely toothed, base of the petiole hollow or concave and covering the bud; outer bark scaling off exposing the inner whitish bark; fruit about an inch in diameter, globose and consisting of a cluster of hairy nutlets on a long, drooping stalk. New England, west to southern Ontario and Wisconsin, south to Florida and Texas. Buttonwood, Planetree, Sycamore. *Platanus occidentalis* L. Fig. 52.
2. Leaves not resembling maple leaves but with 2-4 or more lobes variously arranged and with at least the two lowest veins going to the leaf lobes. *Go to the next key.*

1. Leaf lobes and margins sharply single- or doubled-toothed. *Go to page 57.*
2. Leaf lobes and margins not toothed. *Go to page 60.*

1. Fruit a red, oblong cluster of fleshy fruits (multiple) looking somewhat like a raspberry; leaves with 2 or more rounded lobes or simple. apex abruptly pointed, margins sharply or irregularly toothed, under surface pubescent. Small trees from Vermont to southern Ontario and South Dakota, south to Florida and Texas. Red Mulberry. *Morus rubra* L. Fig. 53.

   White Mulberry, *M. alba* is often found as an escape from cultivation. The leaves are not pubescent on the under surface.

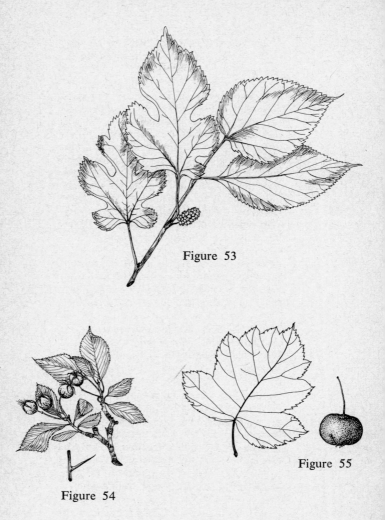

Figure 53

Figure 54

Figure 55

2. Fruits resembling miniature apples; lobes of the leaves sharp-pointed; small trees or shrubs. *Go to the next key.*

1. Small trees or shrubs usually with slender or stout thorns; fruit red or purplish, 3/8 inch or more in diameter and with 1-5 hard nutlets. The Hawthorns. *Crataegus* spp. Fig. 54.
   This is a very large and taxonomically difficult genus belonging to the Rose Family. It is found in nearly all of the Canadian Provinces and the American States.
2. Small trees or shrubs with short, slender, rough, thorn-like branchlets which may bear leaves, flowers and fruit, or, without thorny branchlets; fruits apple-like in cross section. *Go to the next key.*

1. Fruits 1-1 1/2 inches in diameter, greenish; leaves thick, broadest at the base and acute at the apex, upper surface deep green, margins lobed and frequently double-toothed, heart-shaped at the base; spiny branchlets long and slender; calyx persistent on the fruit. New York, southern Ontario, Michigan to Kansas, south to Georgia and Alabama. Wild Sweet Crab Apple. *Pyrus coronaria* L. Fig. 55.
2. Fruit 3/8-5/8 inch in diameter, surface greenish turning yellow or reddish when mature, calyx lobes not persistent on the fruit; leaves oval to lance-like, acute at the apex, lobed or unlobed, margins single- or double-toothed, upper surface dark green, lower surface light green and densely soft pubescent; twigs densely pubescent; branchlets short but not spiny. Small trees or shrubs of the Pacific Coastal Region from southern Alaska to California. Western or Oregon Crab Apple. *Pyrus fusca* Raf. Fig. 56.

1. Leaves 4-lobed with a broad, truncate apex, often with a shallow sinus, each lobe rather pointed, base of the petiole concave and covering the bud; flowers large with 6 conspicuous, light green petals with bright orange bases; fruit a cone of winged seeds (samaras). Vermont, New York, southern Ontario and Michigan, south to Florida and Louisiana. Tulip Tree. *Liriodendron tulipifera* L. Fig. 57.

2. Leaves with two or three lobes or often simple, blade under magnification with translucent dots when held to the light, pubescent on the under surface particularly on the veins, aromatic when bruised; flowers and fruits formed at the tip of the previous year's growth; fruit a blue stone fruit with a red, club-shaped stalk; branchlets green. Southern Maine, west to southern Ontario and Michigan, south and southwest to Florida and Texas. Mitten Tree. Sassafras. *Sassafras albidum* (Nutt.) Nees. Fig. 58.

1. Fruits acorns; lobes of the leaves acute and terminating with bristles, or the lobes rounded and entire. The Oaks. *Quercus* spp. *Go to page 60.*

2. Fruits like miniature apples; lobes of the leaves single- or double-toothed but without bristles. *Go to page 70.*

1. Lobes of the leaves acute and terminating with bristles. *Go to page 60.*

2. Lobes of the leaves rounded and without bristles. *Go to page 63.*

1. Sinuses deep, extending more than 1/2 way to the midrib; acorns small, about 1/2 inch long, cup shallow and covering only the base of the nut; leaves shiny on the upper surface, lower surface with tufts of

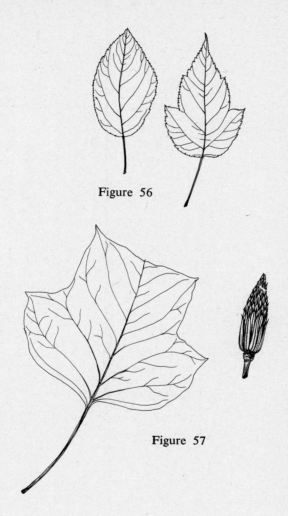

Figure 56

Figure 57

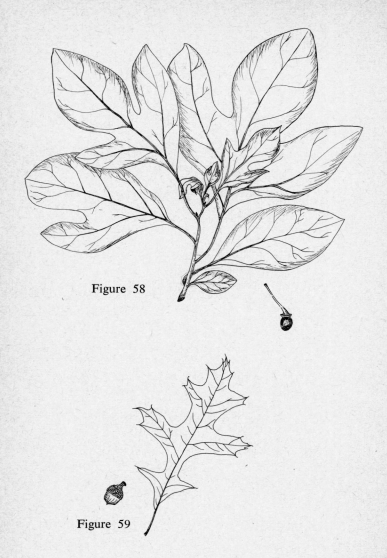

Figure 58

Figure 59

hairs in the axils of the veins. Restricted in distribution to swampy woods New England and New York, the Niagara Peninsula and extreme southwestern Ontario, west to Illinois, south to Virginia and Oklahoma. Pin Oak, Swamp Oak. *Quercus palustris* Muenchh. Fig. 59.

2. Sinuses comparatively shallow and not extending more than 1/2 way to the midrib. *Go to the next key.*

1. Under surface of the leaves with soft, star-shaped hairs particularly in the axils of the veins; leaves oblong with wide sinuses; bracts of the acorns with free tips and the upper ones forming a loose fringe; buds distinctly angled in cross-section and densely hairy. Dry sandy soils southern Maine to southern Ontario and Minnesota, south to Florida and Texas. Black Oak. *Quercus velutina* Lam. Fig. 60

2. Under surface of the leaves without hairs or these only in the axils of the veins; sinuses shallow and not broadly rounded at the base; buds round in cross section; cup scales appressed. Dry and well drained soils from Nova Scotia, to Manitoba, south to Georgia and eastern Oklahoma. Red Oak. *Quercus borealis* Michx. f. Fig. 61.

Two varieties of this species are recognized. The var. *borealis* has a deep acorn cup covering about 1/3 of the acorn, and it is more northern in its distribution. The var. *maxima* (Marsh.) Ashe has a shallow cup covering about 1/4 of the nut, and it is more southern in its distribution.

1. Leaf margins deeply lobed, the middle sinuses at least extending more than 1/3 of the distance to the midrib. *Go to page 64.*
2. Leaf margins with shallow lobes, (in some

species almost tooth-like), the sinuses extending less than 1/3 of the distance to the midrib. *Go to page 67*.

1. Under surface of the leaves without hairs, pale or whitish; leaf blades thin, margins flat; cup covering about 1/4 of the acorn, scales appressed; bark light gray and rough. Upland woods of southern Maine, west to southwestern Quebec, southern Ontario to Minnesota, south to Florida and Texas. White Oak. *Quercus alba* L. Fig. 62.
2. Under surface of the leaves with hairs. *Go to the next key*.

1. Under surface of the leaves with a dense, short, fine, whitish wool of star-shaped hairs; apex of the leaf broad giving an inverted triangular or obovate form to the leaves, apical lobe with shallow or deep sinuses, middle sinuses deep, basal lobes very short and sinuses shallow but reaching almost to the midrib; acorn cup deep, covering 1/2 or more of the nut, scales with long, loose tips and forming a terminal fringe. Rich soils and often on high dry soils from New Brunswick and Maine, west to Manitoba and North Dakota, south to Virginia, Tennessee and Texas. Bur or Mossycup Oak. *Quercus macrocarpa* Michx. Fig. 63.
2. Leaves oblong to obovate, thick, margins slightly turned toward the under surface (revolute), lower surface usually hairy, upper surface glossy, smooth or slightly hairy, lobes terminating with a minute point or callous; acorns about 1 inch long; cup scales with pointed or elongated tips; twigs and petioles hairy. Shrubs to tall, round-topped trees in the Pacific Coastal Region from southwestern British Co-

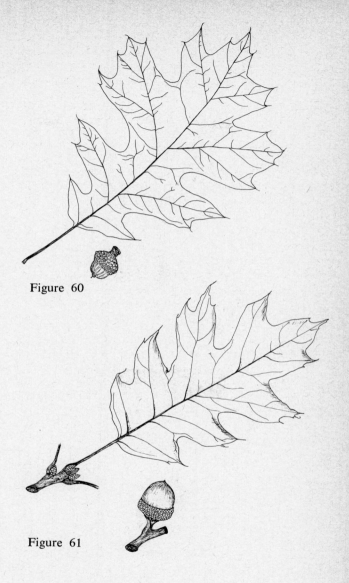

Figure 60

Figure 61

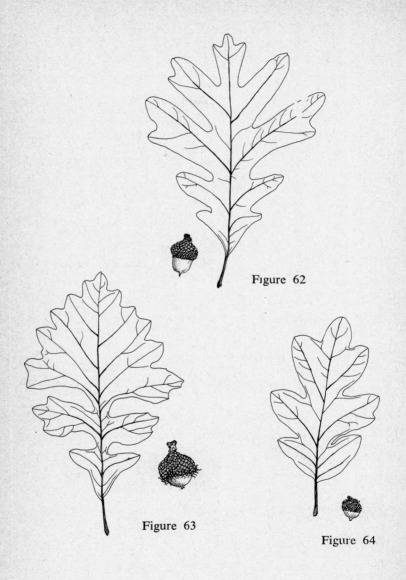

Figure 62

Figure 63

Figure 64

lumbia to California. Western White Oak, Garry Oak, Oregon Oak. *Quercus garryana* Dougl. ex Hook. Fig. 64.

1. Peduncles of the acorns 1-3 inches long and longer than the leaf petioles; leaves obovate, under surface covered with soft, white, star-shaped or branching hairs; cup covering about 1/2 of the nut, upper scales long-pointed and forming a fringe. Moist or swampy soils in southwestern Quebec, southern Ontario, west to Minnesota, and Maine, south to North Carolina and Missouri. Swamp Oak, Swamp White Oak. *Quercus bicolor* Wild. Fig. 65.
2. Acorns sessile or the peduncles not longer than the leaf petioles, bases of the cup scales fused and only the tips free; under surfaces of the leaves densely or slightly pubescent. *Go to the next key.*

1. A shrub; margins of the leaves with 3-7 lobes each, lobes terminating in a callous, under surface densely pubescent; acorn stalks about as long as the leaf stalks. Known from about 3 localities in southern Ontario, and Maine to Minnesota, south to Alabama, and Texas. Dwarf Chestnut or Chinquapin Oak. *Quercus prinoides* Willd. Fig. 66.
2. Trees; margins of the leaves with 8-16 lobes each. *Go to the next key.*

1. Acorns about 1/2-3/4 inch long, sessile or almost so, cup thin, pubescent, covering about 1/2 of the nut; leaves thin, under surface densely pubescent, marginal lobes or teeth rather pointed and directed toward the apex. Vermont, New York, locally in southern Ontario, west to Iowa, south to Florida and Texas. Yellow, Chestnut or Chinquapin Oak. *Quercus muhlenbergii* Engelm. Fig. 67.

67

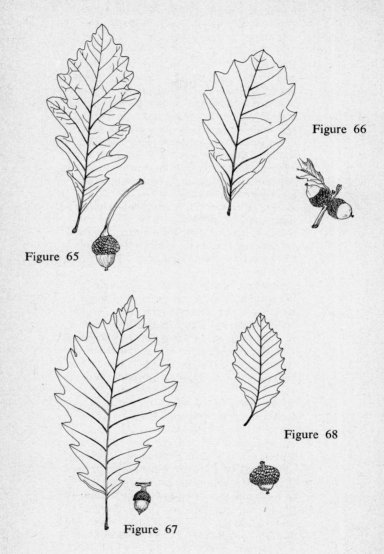

Figure 66

Figure 65

Figure 68

Figure 67

2. Acorns 5/8-1 1/2 inches long, usually on short stalks, cup thick and covering about 1/2 of the nut, upper scale tips long and loose and forming a fringe; leaves thick or somewhat leathery, marginal teeth or lobes rounded. Maine, New York, locally in southern Ontario and Michigan, south to South Carolina and Mississippi. Chestnut Oak. *Quercus prinus* L. Fig. 68.

There are a number of oaks that might be called southern in their distribution which extend their ranges into some of the northern States but are not to be found in Canada. Some of these are:

Scarlet Oak, *Q. coccinea* occurs from Maine, New York and Michigan, south to Georgia and Mississippi, and on the west side of the Mississippi River in Missouri.

Southern Red Oak, *Q. falcata* is an oak of the southern States as far west as Texas and spreading as far north as New York and New Jersey on the Atlantic Coast and in the west to Southern Ohio and Illinois.

The Overcup Oak, *Q. lyrata* extends northward to southern Illinois, Indiana and Delaware.

Swamp Chestnut Oak, *Q. michauxii* is found as far north as Illinois and Indiana and and in the east to New Jersey.

Willow Oak, *Q. phellos* occurs as far north as southern Illinois and on the Coastal Plain north to Pennsylvania and. New Jersey.

Shumard Oak, *Q. shumardii* has its main northern distribution in Ohio, Indiana and southern Illinois and is local northward in Michigan.

Post Oak, *Q. stellata* spreads northward to Iowa and east to Massachusetts.

Shingle Oak, *Q. imbricaria* occurs in dry soils from Michigan and Pennsylvania, south to Kansas and South Carolina.

Jack Oak, *Q. ellipsoidalis* ranges from southern Michigan to Minnesota, south to Missouri.

Black-jack Oak, *Q. marilandica* is a small tree found as far north as southern New York and Michigan to Iowa.

1. Small trees or shrubs usually with slender or stout thorns; fruit red or purplish, 3/8 inch or more in diameter and with 1-5 hard nutlets. The Hawthorns. *Crataegus* spp. See Fig. 54.

    This is a very large and taxonomically difficult genus of shrubs or small trees belonging to the Rose Family. It is found in nearly all of the Canadian Provinces and the American States.

2. Small trees or shrubs with short, slender, rough, thorn-like branchlets which may bear leaves, flowers and fruit, or, without thorny branchlets; fruits applelike in cross section. *Go to the next key*.

1. Fruit 1-1 1/2 inches in diameter, greenish; leaves thick, broadest at the base and acute at the apex, upper surface deep green, margin lobed or unlobed and doubly toothed, heart-shaped at the base; spiny branchlets long and slender. Open woods, fields New York, southern Ontario, Michigan to Kansas, south to Georgia and Alabama. Wild Sweet Crab Apple. *Pyrus coronaria* L. Fig. 55.

2. Fruit 3/8-5/8 inch in diameter, surface greenish turning yellow or reddish when mature, calyx lobes not persistent on the fruit; leaves oval to lance-like, acute at the apex, lobed or unlobed, margins single- or double-toothed, .upper surface dark green, lower surface light green and densely soft pubescent; twigs densely pubescent. Small trees or shrubs of the Pacific Coastal Re-

gion from southern Alaska to California. Western or Oregon Crab Apple. *Pyrus fusca* Raf. Fig. 56.

1. Margins of the leaves entire or some of the leaves on the same tree with lobes or enlarged teeth. *Go to page 71.*
2. Margins of the leaves wavy (undulate) or toothed. *Go to page 79.*

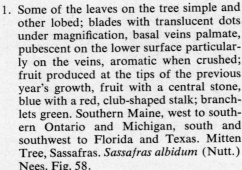

1. Some of the leaves on the tree simple and others lobed or with few, obvious, enlarged teeth. *Go to page 71.*
2. None of the leaves on the tree lobed. *Go to page 72.*

1. Some of the leaves on the tree simple and other lobed; blades with translucent dots under magnification, basal veins palmate, pubescent on the lower surface particularly on the veins, aromatic when crushed; fruit produced at the tips of the previous year's growth, fruit with a central stone, blue with a red, club-shaped stalk; branchlets green. Southern Maine, west to southern Ontario and Michigan, south and southwest to Florida and Texas. Mitten Tree, Sassafras. *Sassafras albidum* (Nutt.) Nees. Fig. 58.
2. Some of the leaves with entire margins and others with distant, pointed projections or enlarged teeth near the apex, leaves tending to be clustered at the ends of short branches, blades rather thick, oval or broadest above the middle (obovate), often pubescent on the veins of the lower surface, somewhat glossy on the upper surface; flowers and fruits produced on stalks arising in the axils of the leaves, fruit dark blue and with a central pit or stone. Maine, New York, southern Ontario and Michigan, south to Florida and Texas.

Pepperidge, Sour Gum, Tupelo. *Nyssa sylvatica* Marsh. Fig. 69.

1. Fruits large and fleshy; leaves large, up to 12 inches long. *Go to page 72*.
2. Fruits not large, consisting of bean-like pods, berries or arranged in catkins; leaves less than 6 inches long. *Go to page 74*.

1. Leaves up to 10 or 12 inches long, broadest near the apex, abruptly pointed, tapering to the base, leaf stalk short, leaves with a disagreeable odour when crushed; flowers purplish or maroon and appearing on the previous year's growth and before the leaves open; fruits green at first but becoming brownish, large and fleshy and containing flattened seeds about 1 inch long, fruit edible. A small tree from New York, Niagara Peninsula and counties of southwestern Ontario, Michigan and Nebraska, south to Florida and Texas. Often planted. Pawpaw. *Asimina triloba* (L.) Dunal. Fig. 70.
2. Leaves 4 or more inches long, oval in outline, light green and usually soft pubescent on the lower surface; flowers large and greenish; fruit a fleshy cone, reddish, oblique at the base and curved; when mature each fruit splits open exposing a fleshy, red seed attached by a slender white thread. A large tree. Western New York, locally in southern Ontario, southwest to Arkansas and Oklahoma, south to Georgia and Alabama. Magnolia, Cucumber Tree. *Magnolia acuminata* L. Fig. 71.
   Several other less widely distributed species extend northward to southern Ohio, Pennsylvania and Virginia.

Common Persimmon, *Diospyros virginiana* L. would belong to the trees with the char-

1. *Red Maple in Autumn*

4. *American Chestnut, fruit*

2. *White Birch, bark*

5. *Redbud, flowers*

3. *White Birch Stand*

6. *Dogwood, flowers*

7. *Hawthorn, fruit*

10. *Tulip Tree, flower*

8. *Beech, fruit and bud*

11. *Tulip Tree, fruit*

9. *Witch Hazel, leaves and fruit*

12. *Magnolia, fruit*

13. *Sycamore, bark*

14. *Red Oak, fruit (acorns)*

15. *Oak in winter*

17. *Sassafras, leaves*

16. *Staghorn Sumac,
fruit*

18. *Sassafras, fruit*

19. *Mountain Ash, fruit*

22. *American Yew, fruit*

20. *White Elm in Winter*

23. *White Cedar*

21. *Ponderosa or Bull
    Pine*

24. *Ironwood, leaves
    and fruit*

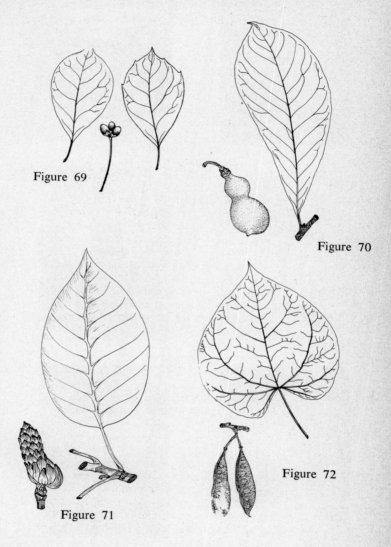

Figure 69

Figure 70

Figure 71

Figure 72

acteristics of this section of the key. The bark
is dark and thick forming thick, square, scaly
plates; leaves are oval to oblong, from 3-6
inches long; fruit a large, yellowish, edible
berry up to 1 1/2 inches thick. Its main distribution is in the river flats of the lower
Mississippi river basin and the Atlantic
Coastal Plain. It comes northward from
Florida and Texas to Missouri, Illinois, east
to Connecticut.

1. Small trees; leaves rounded, heart-shaped
   at the base, palmately veined, slightly pubescent on the lower surface or glabrous;
   flowers pinkish or purplish and pea-or
   bean-like, appearing on the branches of
   former years' growth before the leaves;
   fruit a flat, bean-like pod up to 3 1/2
   inches long. Connecticut, Pennsylvania,
   reported once from Pelee Islands Ontario,
   southern Michigan to Iowa and Nebraska,
   south to Florida and Texas. Redbud,
   Judas Tree. *Cercis canadensis* L. Fig. 72.

2. Leaves oval, oblong or elliptical; fruits not
   bean-like pods but berry-like or arranged
   in catkins. *Go to the next key.*

1. Fruits berry-like and usually present during the summer and early fall. *Go to page
   74.*
2. Fruits capsules arranged in catkins and absent during the summer and fall. Willow.
   Salix spp. *Go to page 77.*

1. Leaves persistent, oval or oblong, thick
   and leathery, shiny on the upper surface,
   pale and glaucous on the lower surface
   and reticulate, margins revolute, entire or
   slightly toothed; fruits orange or reddish
   and somewhat berry-like, about 1/2 inch
   in diameter; older bark reddish and peeling off the trunks and branches leaving the
   bright, reddish inner bark. Small trees of

the Pacific Coastal Region from south-western British Columbia to California. Madrona, Arbutus. *Arbutus menziesii* Pursh. Fig. 73.

2. Leaves deciduous, not leathery. *Go to the next key.*

1. Leaf veins prominent, extending to the leaf margins; leaves 2-7 inches long, broadly elliptical to oblong with a rounded apex and a very small apical point, margins very finely and obscurely toothed, under surface with a velvety, short pubescence, veins with brownish hairs; twigs with yellowish or brownish pubescence; fruit purplish or black and berry-like, about 3/8 inch in diameter. Small trees or shrubs of the Pacific Coastal Region from British Columbia to California and occasionally inland in British Columbia, Idaho and Montana. Cascara, Cascara Buckthorn. *Rhamnus purshiana* DC. Fig. 74.

2. Leaf veins branching before reaching the leaf margins. *Go to the next key.*

1. Flowers and fruits in the axils of the leaves, fruits dark blue and with a central pit or stone; leaves 1 1/2-5 inches long, rather thick, oval or broadest above the middle (obovate), margins often with enlarged, toothed projections near the apex, often pubescent on the lower veins, somewhat glossy on the upper surface, tending to be clustered at the ends of the short twigs. Maine, New York, southern Ontario and Michigan, south to Florida and Texas. Pepperidge, Sour Gum, Tupelo. *Nyssa sylvatica* Marsh. Fig. 69.

2. Flowers and fruits in flat-topped, branching clusters (cymes) at the ends of the branches, fruit a small, blue, stone fruit about 1/4 inch in diameter and borne on short, red stalks; leaves clustered at the

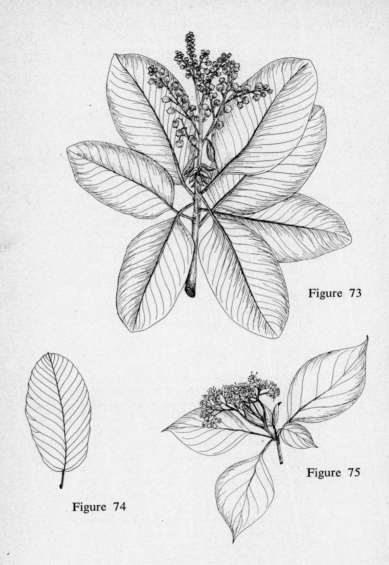

Figure 73

Figure 74

Figure 75

ends of the branches or branchlets, alternate but sometime appearing as if opposite or whorled, pinnately veined, veins prominent and arching toward the apex, slightly pubescent on the lower surface; branches greenish and with a white pith. Small trees or shrubs from Newfoundland and Nova Scotia to Manitoba and Minnesota, south to Florida and Arkansas. Alternate-leaved Dogwood, Pagoda Dogwood. *Cornus alternifolia* L. f. Fig. 75.

1. Leaves pubescent on both surfaces but more densely so on the lower surface; twigs soft-pubescent; leaves broadest above the middle and tapering to the base, apex rounded and abruptly pointed, teeth, if present, merely glandular or calloused points. Chiefly in the Pacific Coastal Region from Alaska to California. Sitka or Satin Willow. *Salix sitchensis* Sanson. Fig. 76.
2. Leaves pubescent on the lower surface only. *Go to the next key.*

1. Leaves oblong, elliptical or broadly club-shaped (clavate), apex short-pointed, margins occasionally slightly toothed, upper surface dark green and glabrous, under surface whitish and from slightly to densely pubescent, pubescence often brownish. Manitoba to British Columbia and Alaska, south to California and New Mexico. Western Black Willow, Scouler Willow. *Salix scouleriana* Barratt. Fig. 77.
2. Leaves elliptical or oblong, abruptly pointed at the apex, under surface often very veiny (reticulate) or roughened, silvery or bluish and with grayish or brownish hairs; branchlets grayish-pubescent. Small trees or shrubs across Canada and the northern States. Beak Willow, Bebb's Willow. *Salix bebbiana* Sarg. Fig. 78.

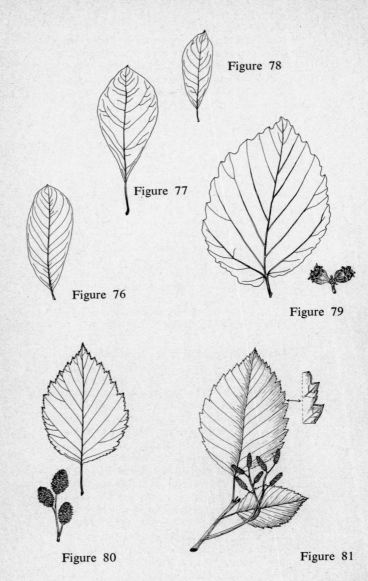

Figure 78

Figure 77

Figure 76

Figure 79

Figure 80

Figure 81

1. Margins of the leaves wavy or undulate (sinuate), with or without teeth, sometimes, as in Oaks, the undulations may become almost large teeth. *Go to page 79.*
2. Margins of the leaves all distinctly toothed. *Go to page 83.*

1. Base of the leaf asymmetrical, under surface slightly hairy, blade pinnately veined, oval or almost orbicular or obovate, margins wavy or with rounded lobes; terminal buds stalked, without scales but with a yellowish or brown pubescence of jointed or star-shaped hairs; flowers in the axils of the leaves, yellow and appearing in September or October of one year and the fruit maturing the following autumn; fruit a 2-celled capsule opening at the apex with some force and shooting out the seeds. Small trees or shrubs Nova Scotia, southwestern Quebec, southern Ontario to Minnesota, south to Florida and Texas. Witch Hazel. *Hamamelis virginiana* L. Fig. 79.

2. Base of the leaf symmetrical or almost so. *Go to the next key.*

1. Fruits acorns; leaves tapering to the base, undulations or small lobes without small teeth. Oaks. *Quercus* spp. *Go to page 79.*
2. Fruits small, woody cones; leaves rounded at the base, undulations toothed. Alders. *Alnus* spp. *Go to page 81.*

1. Peduncles of the acorns 1-3 inches long and longer than the leaf petioles; leaves obovate, under surface covered with soft, white, star-shaped or branching hairs; cup covering about 1/3 of the nut, upper scales long-pointed and forming a fringe. Moist or swampy soils in southwestern Quebec, southern Ontario, west to Minnesota, and

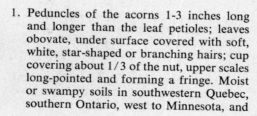

Maine, south to North Carolina and Missouri. Swamp Oak, Swamp White Oak. *Quercus bicolor*. Willd. Fig. 65.

2. Acorns sessile or the peduncles not longer than the leaf petioles, bases of the cup scales fused and only the tips free; under surfaces of the leaves densely or slightly pubescent. *Go to the next key*.

1. A shrub; margins of the leaves with 3-7 lobes each, lobes terminating in a callous, under surface densely pubescent; acorn stalks about as long as the leaf stalks. Known from about 3 localities in southern Ontario, and Maine to Minnesota, south to Alabama and Texas. Dwarf Chestnut or Chinquapin Oak. *Quercus prinoides* Wild. Fig. 66.

2. Trees; margins of the leaves with 8-18 lobes each. *Go to the next key*.

1. Acorns about 1/2-3/4 inch long, sessile or almost so, cup thin, pubescent, covering about 1/2 of the nut; leaves thin, under surface densely pubescent, marginal lobes or teeth pointed and directed toward the apex. Rather scattered in its distribution on dry soils and river flats in Vermont, New York, locally in southern Ontario, west to Iowa, south to Florida and Texas, Yellow, Chestnut or Chinquapin Oak. *Quercus muhlenbergii* Engelm. Fig. 67.

2. Acorns 5/8-1 1/2 inches long, usually on short stalks, cup thick and covering about 1/2 of the nut, upper scale tips long and loose and forming a fringe; leaves thick or somewhat leathery, marginal teeth oi lobes rounded, under surface slightly pubescent. Maine, New York, locally in southern Ontario and Michigan, south to South Carolina and Mississippi. Chestnut Oak. *Quercus prinus* L. Fig. 68.

1. Flowers and fruits developing on the twigs of the new season's growth and flowers opening with the expanding of the leaves; terminal buds sessile and sharp-pointed; nutlets winged; under surface of the leaves slightly pubescent particularly on the veins and in the vein axils, upper surface glabrous; young twigs with numerous unstalked glands; sweet-scented. In the Pacific Coastal Region from Alaska to California, east to the Rocky Mountains and south to Colorado. Sitka Alder. *Alnus sinuata* (Regel) Rydb. Fig. 80.

2. Flowers and fruits developing on the twigs of last year's growth and flowers opening early in the spring before the leaves. *Go to the next key.*

1. Leaf margins rolled toward the lower surface (revolute), lower surface soft, gray to brownish pubescent and glandular dotted, veins rusty coloured, both apex and base somewhat tapering; nutlets distinctly winged. Trees of the Pacific Coastal Region from Alaska to California. Red Alder. *Alnus rubra* Bong. Fig. 81.

2. Leaf margins not rolled or revolute, under surface pubescent particularly on the veins and reticulate, light green in colour; nutlets without an evident wing. Speckled Alder. *Alnus rugosa* (DuRoi) Spreng. Fig. 82.

Some consider *A. rugosa* to be the eastern species of a very confusing species complex. *A. incana* (L.) Moench., is described by Hitchcock *et al* to include *A. rugosa* and *A. tenuifolia* Nutt. The latter species has also been thought to be a separate species in southwestern Alberta and eastern British Columbia. The species complex ranges from Newfoundland and Nova Scotia to British Columbia and

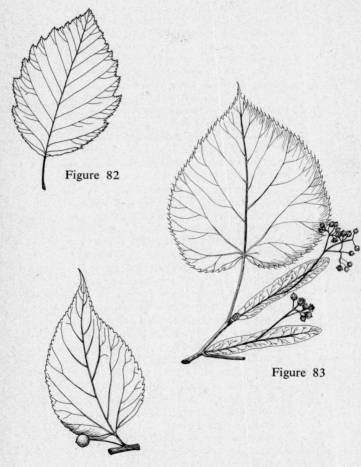

Figure 82

Figure 83

Figure 84

Alaska, south to California, New Mexico and northeast to Pennsylvania and Maryland.

1. Leaves distinctly asymmetrical at the base, margins single- or double-toothed or serrate. *Go to page 83.*
2. Leaves symmetrical at the base or almost so, margins single- or double-toothed or serrate. *Go to page 86.*

1. Leaves rather rounded, about as broad as long, heart-shaped at the base, teeth sharp, glandular- or callous-tipped; under surface without star-shaped hairs at maturity; smooth, reddish winter buds not central on the leaf scar; flowers and fruits in branching, axillary clusters, peduncle with a bract or wing, fruit nut-like and pubescent. Rich upland woods from New Brunswick to Manitoba, south to North Carolina, Tennessee and Oklahoma. Basswood, American Linden. *Tilia americana* L. Fig. 83.

White Basswood, *Tilia heterophylla* is found chiefly in the Appalachian region from southern Pennsylvania to Indiana, south to Florida and Alabama. It also crosses the Mississippi River into Missouri and Arkansas.

The under surface of the leaves are covered with star-shaped hairs.

2. Leaves more or less oval or ovate, longer than broad. *Go to the next key.*

1. Leaves broadest below the middle and tapering abruptly to a slender apex, asymmetrical at the base, teeth simple and rather rounded, basal veins palmate; flowers and fruits arising from the axils of the leaves, fruit a stone fruit, black, blue or reddish; bark grayish and with warty, corky ridges. Rich moist or dry soils or

rocky ground from Southwestern Quebec, southern Ontario to North Dakota, south to New Hampshire and Vermont to Georgia and Oklahoma. Hackberry. *Celtis occidentalis* L. Fig. 84.

2. Leaves broadest near the middle; veining pinnate and most of the veins not dividing at the leaf margins; fruits winged. The Elms. *Ulmus* spp. *Go to the next key.*

1. Upper surface of the leaf very rough, lower surface with a short, appressed pubescence, margins double-toothed, teeth calloused; branchlets pubescent; upper part of the tree not widely branching and branches slender and short; buds reddish and pubescent; flowers and fruits very short-stalked; winged fruit about 3/4 inch long and pubescent over the seed area only; wing margin not ciliate. Moist woods and soils Maine, southwestern Quebec and Ontario to Lake Superior, south and southwest to Florida and Texas. Red or Slippery Elm. *Ulmus rubra* Muhl. Fig. 85.

2. Upper leaf surface smooth or very slightly roughened; margins of the samaras with a hairy fringe (ciliate). *Go to the next key.*

1. Trunks of the trees continuous to well above the middle, branches drooping and with stout, corky ridges; fruit about 3/4 inch long and the whole surface pubescent, margins ciliate; leaves pubescent on the lower surface particularly on the veins. New England, New York, southwestern Quebec, southern Ontario, west to Minnesota, south to Tennessee and Arkansas. Found locally in a number of States. Rock or Cork Elm. *Ulmus thomasi* Sarg. Fig. 86.

2. Trunks of the trees dividing into several large branches, ultimate branchlets, drooping and giving an umbrella-like appear-

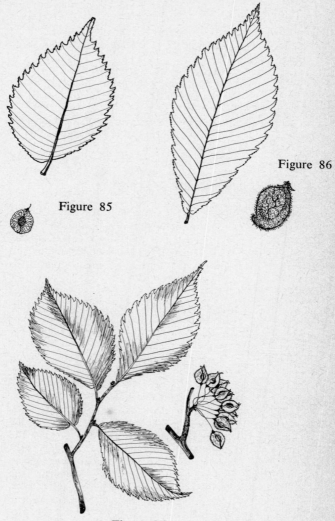

Figure 85

Figure 86

Figure 87

ance to the crown; winged fruits about 1/2 inch long, surface glabrous but the margin ciliate. Nova Scotia to Saskatchewan, south to Florida and Texas. White or American Elm. *Ulmus americana* L. Fig. 87.

This species is fast disappearing from our landscape because of its susceptibility to the Dutch Elm disease.

1. Nearly all the main veins of the leaf readily traceable to the leaf margins. *Go to page 86.*
2. Nearly all of the main veins of the leaf disappearing before reaching the leaf margin. *Go to page 96.*

1. Teeth on the margins of the leaves simple but often irregular. *Go to page 86.*
2. Teeth on the margins of the leaves double, or with the large teeth or sinuations followed by one or more smaller teeth. *Go to page 89.*

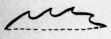

1. Large trees; fruits spiny or bur-like nuts. *Go to page 86.*
2. Trees or shrubs; fruits not bur-like or spiny but berry-like or arranged in catkins. *Go to page 88.*

1. Teeth of the leaf margins short and straight; fruit small and bur-like and containing 2, triangular or pyramidal nuts; leaves 2 1/2-4 inches long, veins of the under surface pubescent; buds slender and cylindrical and about 1 inch long; bark smooth and gray. Rich upland woods from Nova Scotia to Ontario, Michigan and Wisconsin, south to Florida and Texas. Common Beech. *Fagus grandifolia* Ehrh. Fig. 88.
2. Teeth of the leaf margins long and curving

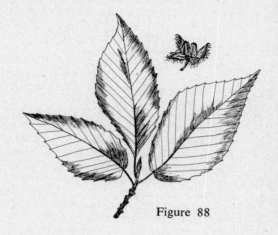

Figure 88

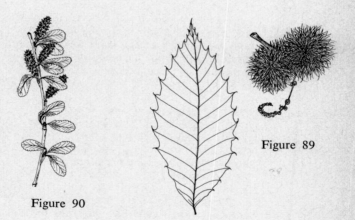

Figure 90

Figure 89

toward the leaf apex, apex long-pointed; leaves 6 or more inches long; fruit a globular, spiny bur about 2 inches in diameter. American Chestnut. *Castanea dentata* (Marsh.) Borkh. Fig. 89.

This was once a common tree in southern Ontario and the eastern States, but the Chestnut Blight has eliminated practically all mature trees and only small, shrubby trees or suckers are to be seen.

1. Fruits berry-like, purplish or black, about 3/8 inch in diameter; leaf veins prominent and extending to the leaf margins; leaves 2-7 inches long, broadly elliptical to oblong with a rounded apex and a very small apical point, margins very finely and obscurely toothed, under surface with a short, soft pubescence, veins with brownish hairs; twigs with yellowish or brownish pubescence. Small trees or shrubs of the Pacific Coastal Region from British Columbia to California and occasionally in the interior of British Columba to Idaho and Montana. Cascara, Cascara Buckthorn. *Rhamnus purshiana* DC. Fig. 74.

2. Fruits arranged in catkins. *Go to the next key.*

1. Erect or prostrate shrubs; flowers and fruits in tight catkins; leaves small, more or less rounded, coarsely toothed, veins and veinlets prominent (reticulate); twigs more or less pubescent and often glandular. *Go to page 88.*

2. Small trees or occasionally with large trunks; flowers and fruits in open or loose catkins with bladder-like or wing-like bracts. *Go to page 89.*

1. Twigs and leaves without resin glands or with very few of them; leaves thin, light green on the under surface. Swampy or

marsh ground from Newfoundland and Nova Scotia to Ontario and Michigan, south to Maryland and Indiana. Swamp Birch. *Betula pumila* L. Fig. 90.

2. Twigs and leaves with numerous resinous glands; leaves more or less leathery and glutinous, green on both surfaces. Swampy or marshy ground across Canada and north to Alaska, south to California in the west and to Maine and New Hampshire in the east. Dwarf Birch. *Betula glandulosa* Michx.

1. Fertile flowers and fruits in a terminal, whitish raceme with silvery hairs at the base of each inflated flower bract; fruits enclosed in the enlarged, bladdery flower bracts; leaves oblong or oval, tapering at the apex, sharply single- or double-toothed, slightly pubescent on the under surface; bark grayish and in narrow, scaly ridges. New Brunswick to Manitoba, south to Florida and Texas. Ironwood, Hop Hornbeam. *Ostrya virginiana* (Mill.) K. Koch. Fig. 91.

2. Fertile flowers and fruits in terminal racemes and in the axils of flat, 3-lobed flower bracts; bark grayish, fluted, smooth and resembling greatly the bark of the Common Beech; leaves oblong or oval, tapering to a sharp apex and with small, sharp teeth, often double-toothed. Southwestern Quebec to Manitoba and Minnesota, south to Florida and Texas. Blue Beech, American Hornbeam. *Carpinus caroliniana* Walt. Fig. 92.

1. Trees or shrubs of rather moist habitats; fruits in catkins forming woody, persistent cones, cone bracts 3-5 lobed. *Go to page 91.*

2. Fruiting catkins not forming woody cones; fruit bracts deciduous. *Go to page 92.*

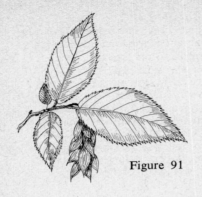

Figure 91

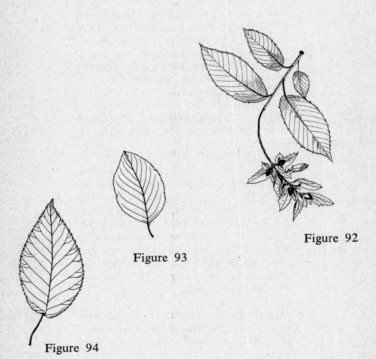

Figure 92

Figure 93

Figure 94

1. Flowers and fruits developing on the twigs of the new season's growth and flowers opening with the expanding of the leaves; terminal buds sessile and sharp-pointed; nutlets winged; under surface of the leaves slightly pubescent, particularly in the axils of the veins, upper surface glabrous; young twigs with numerous, unstalked glands; sweet scented. In the Pacific Coastal Region from Alaska to California, east to the Rocky Mountains and south to Colorado. Sitka Alder. *Alnus sinuata* (Regel) Rydb. Fig. 80.

2. Flowers and fruits developing on the twigs of last season's growth and flowering early in the spring before the expanding of the leaves. *Go to the next key.*

1. Leaf margins without the undulations or lobes but finely single- or double-toothed; lower surface pubescent or slightly so; young growth pubescent or smooth; nutlets without a distinct wing. Southern British Columbia and the adjacent States south to California. White Alder. *Alnus rhombifolia* Nutt. Fig. 93.

2. Leaf margins with the undulations or lobes. *Go to the next key.*

1. Leaf margins rolled toward the lower surface (revolute), lower surface soft pubescent and glandular dotted, veins rusty coloured, both apex and base slightly pointed; nutlets distinctly winged. Pacific Coastal Region from Alaska to California. Red Alder. *Alnus rubra* Bong. Fig. 81.

2. Leaf margins not revolute; under surface pubescent particularly on the veins and reticulate, light green in colour; nutlets without evident wings. Trans-Canada in its distribution. Speckled Alder. *Alnus rugosa* (DuRoi) Spreng. *See* Fig. 82 and note on page *81.*

1. Fruits in compact catkins with the bracts small, thin, entire or 3-lobed and deciduous. *Go to page 92.*
2. Fruits in open or loose catkins with bladder-like or large, 3-lobed, wing-like bracts. Ironwood and Blue Beech. *Go to page 95.*

1. Catkins erect or horizontal, short and stout; inner bark of the trunk and twigs with a wintergreen odour and flavour. *Go to page 92.*
2. Catkins often pendulous or drooping when mature, slender, longer than broad; bark odourless and tasteless. *Go to page 92.*

1. Bark brownish, forming thick plates on the trunks, not at all papery; scales of the fruiting catkins not pubescent; leaves with finely, double-toothed margins, sharply pointed apex and slightly heart-shaped base. At one time well known in parts of southwestern Quebec and southern Ontario, now rare in both provinces, New England and New York, west to Ohio, south through the Appalachians to Georgia and Alabama. Cherry, Sweet or Black Birch. *Betula lenta* L. Fig. 94.
2. Bark light brown or silvery-gray, forming thin, curly sheets easily peeled from the trunk; scales of the fruiting catkins pubescent; leaf margins coarsely double-toothed, base not heart-shaped, apex tapering to a rather long tip. Moist woods from Newfoundland and Nova Scotia to Ontario, south to Ohio and Indiana and through the Appalachians to Georgia. Yellow Birch. *Betula lutea* Michx. f. Fig. 95.

1. Bark more or less glossy-white to faintly orange-coloured and peeling readily into

horizontal sheets, inner bark orange-coloured; under surface of the leaves light green, pubescent on the veins or with tufts of hairs in the axils of the veins, upper surface dark green; leaf apex not long-tapering. Across Canada and north to Yukon and Alaska, south to Washington, Minnesota, Wisconsin and Pennsylvania. Local in a number of other States. White, Paper or Canoe Birch. *Betula papyrifera* Marsh. Fig. 96.

2. Outer bark not peeling. *Go to the next key*.

1. Outer bark chalky-white and dull, occasionally pinkish, whiteness coming off on the fingers when the trunk is rubbed; trunks with conspicuous, black, decurrent lines at the angles of the branches; leaf blade triangular with a long, tapering apex, teeth with calloused apices; upper surface often shiny, under surface not pubescent; branchlets often with wart-like glands. Small trees with a single trunk or 2 or more trunks together. Open woods and fields from Nova Scotia to eastern Ontario, south to Pennsylvania and Indiana. Old-field or Gray Birch. *Betula populifolia* Marsh. Fig. 97.

This species hybridies with the Paper Birch, *B. papyrifera*, and trees showing intermediate characteristics are not un-common.

2. Bark of the small trees or shrubs not white but reddish or brownish. *Go to the next key*.

1. Small trees or shrubs, usually in clumps; bark red and shining; twigs covered with clear, resinous glands and slightly hairy; leaves oval, mostly about 1 1/2 inches long, pointed at the apex, glandular, particularly on the lower surface and on the petioles, no tufts of hairs in the axils of the

Figure 95

Figure 96

Figure 97

Figure 99

Figure 98

veins on the under surface; wing of the fruit about as broad as the pubescent seed body. Low, moist lake and river margins or wet soils. from Manitoba to British Columbia and Alaska, south to California, the Dakotas and New Mexico. River Birch. *Betula occidentalis* Hook. Fig. 98.

2. Erect or prostrate shrubs; leaves small, more or less rounded, coarsely toothed, veins and veinlets prominent (reticulate); twigs more or less pubescent or glandular. *Go to the next key*.

1. Twigs and leaves without resin glands or with very few glands; leaves thin, light green on the under surface. Swampy or marshy ground from Newfoundland and Nova Scotia to Ontario and Michigan, south to Maryland and Indiana. Swamp Birch. *Betula pumila* L. Fig. 90.

2. Twigs and leaves with numerous resin glands; leaves more or less leathery and gutinous, green on both surfaces. Swampy or marshy ground across Canada and north to Alaska, south to California in the west and to Maine and New Hampshire in the east. Dwarf Birch. *Betula glandulosa* Michx.

1. Fertile flowers and fruits in a terminal, whitish raceme with silvery hairs at the base of each inflated flower bract; fruits enclosed in the enlarged, bladdery flower bracts; leaves oblong or oval, tapering at the apex, sharply single- or double-toothed, slightly pubescent on the under surface; bark grayish and in narrow, scaly ridges. New Brunswick to Manitoba, south to Florida and Texas. Ironwood, Hop Hornbeam. *Ostrya virginiana* (Mill.) K. Koch. Fig. 91.

2. Fertile flowers and fruits in terminal ra-

cemes and in the axils of large, flat, three-lobed flower bracts; bark grayish, fluted, smooth and resembling greatly the bark of the Common Beech; leaves oblong or oval, tapering to a sharp apex and with small, sharp teeth, often double-toothed. Southwestern Quebec to Manitoba and Minnesota, south to Florida and Texas. Blue Beech, American Hornbeam. *Carpinus caroliniana* Walt. Fig. 92.

1. Fruits red and berry-like, somewhat resembling a raspberry; leaves simple or with 2 or more lobes, margins sharply and irregularly toothed, under surface pubescent. Small trees from Vermont to southern Ontario and South Dakota, south to Florida and Texas. Red Mulberry. *Morus rubra* L. Fig. 53.

   The introduced, and often escaped, White Mulberry, *M. alba*, lacks pubescence on the under surface of the leaves, or this occurring only on the veins; the fruit may be white, pink or almost black.
2. Fruits not berry-like. *Go to the next key*.

1. Fruits arranged in catkins, if present, but the capsules mature early in the spring and are usually absent when the leaves are mature. Included here are the Poplars and Willows. Poplars may be recognized by the presence of a smooth, greenish or grayish bark which usually will be found on some part of the trunk or branches, and the buds have several bud scales. Willow bark is variable in characteristics, they grow most frequently in moist or wet habitats, and the buds are appressed to the twigs and have only one bud scale. *Go to page 102*.
2. Fruits resembling miniature apples, or cherries or plums. *Go to the next key*.

1. Fruits small and apple-like. *Go to page 97.*
2. Fruits resembling small cherries or plums; leaf petioles usually with one or more glands near their apex, except in *Prunus americana*, Wild Plum. *Go to page 98.*

1. Trees or shrubs without thorns, very variable in their characteristics and often difficult to separate into species; leaves oval or elliptical, usually finely toothed; flowers and fruits in racemes; fruits reddish or purplish. June-berry, Shadbush, Service-berry. Among those that may become tree-like are *Amelanchier alnifolia* Nutt. (*A. florida*); A. *arborea* (Michx. f.) Fern.; *A. canadensis* (L.) Medic. and *A. laevis* Wieg. Fig. 99.
2. Small trees or shrubs with true thorns or thorn-like branchlets. *Go to the next key.*

1. Small trees or shrubs usually with slender or stout thorns; fruit red or purplish, 1/2 inch or more in diameter and with 1-5 hard nutlets. The Hawthorns. *Crataegus* spp. Fig. 54 and note on page 59.
2. Small trees or shrubs with short, slender, rough, thorn-like branchlets which may bear leaves, flowers and fruit, or, without thorny branchlets; fruits apple-like in cross section. *Go to the next key.*

1. Fruit 1-1 1/2 inches in diameter, greenish; leaves thick, broadest at the base and acute at the apex, upper surface deep green, margin lobed or unlobed and single- or double-toothed, heart-shaped at the base; spiny branchlets long and slender. New York, southern Ontario, Michigan to Kansas, south to Georgia and Alabama. Wild Sweet Crab Apple. *Pyrus coronaria* L. Fig. 55.

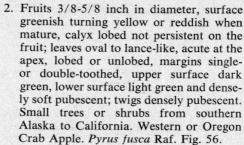

2. Fruits 3/8-5/8 inch in diameter, surface greenish turning yellow or reddish when mature, calyx lobed not persistent on the fruit; leaves oval to lance-like, acute at the apex, lobed or unlobed, margins single- or double-toothed, upper surface dark green, lower surface light green and densely soft pubescent; twigs densely pubescent. Small trees or shrubs from southern Alaska to California. Western or Oregon Crab Apple. *Pyrus fusca* Raf. Fig. 56.

1. Fruits plum-like; stone flattened or lenticular; branches with short, sharp, spine-like branchlets. *Go to page 98.*
2. Fruits cherry-like, stone globose; branches without spiny branchlets. *Go to page 98.*

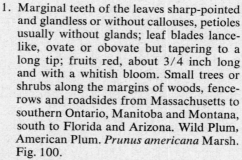

1. Marginal teeth of the leaves sharp-pointed and glandless or without callouses, petioles usually without glands; leaf blades lance-like, ovate or obovate but tapering to a long tip; fruits red, about 3/4 inch long and with a whitish bloom. Small trees or shrubs along the margins of woods, fence-rows and roadsides from Massachusetts to southern Ontario, Manitoba and Montana, south to Florida and Arizona. Wild Plum, American Plum. *Prunus americana* Marsh. Fig. 100.

2. Marginal teeth rounded and with glandular or calloused tips; leaf blade lance-like, or oval with a long-pointed apex, petioles with glands; fruit red, oval, about 3/4 inch long and with a slight whitish bloom. Small trees or shrubs from New Brunswick to Manitoba and South Dakota, south to New England, Georgia, Illinois and Iowa. Canada Plum. *Prunus nigra* Ait. Fig. 101.

1. Flowers or fruits in long racemes. *Go to page 99.*

2. Flowers or fruits in umbels or short, clustered corymbs. *Go to page 99*.

1. Frequently large trees, bark of older trees black and scaly, inner bark aromatic; leaves with appressed, blunt teeth which are callous-tipped, blades contracted to a long, tapering tip, lower midrib often pubescent near the base. Upland woods from Nova Scotia to Ontario and Minnesota, south to Florida, Texas and Arizona. Black Cherry. *Prunus serotina* Ehrh. Fig. 102.

2. Usually small trees or shrubs with a tight bark; leaves with sharp somewhat spreading teeth, not callous-tipped, apex abruptly pointed. Newfoundland and Nova Scotia to British Columbia, south to Tennessee and California. Choke Cherry. *Prumus virginiana* L. Fig. 103.

1. Flowers and fruits in umbellate clusters; leaves elliptical, apex taper-pointed and often curved; margins with sharp or rounded, irregular teeth slightly callous-tipped. Small trees or shrubs from Newfoundland and Nova Scotia to British Columbia, south to Tennessee and Colorado. Bird or Pin Cherry. *Prunus pensylvanica* L. f. Fig. 104.

2. Flowers and fruits in short, branching clusters (corymbs); leaves elliptical, broadest about the middle or slightly obovate, marginal teeth rounded and with pointed glands or callouses, base of the leaf blade with glands but usually none on the petiole, under surface pubescent; branches and twigs more or less pubescent. Shrubs or small trees from southern British Columbia to California and Arizona. Bitter Cherry. *Prunus emarginata* (Dougl.) Walpers. Fig. 105.

Figure 100

Figure 101

Figure 102

Figure 103

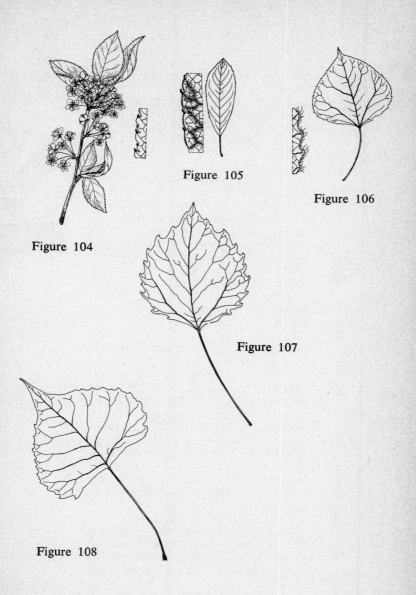

Figure 104

Figure 105

Figure 106

Figure 107

Figure 108

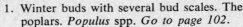

1. Winter buds with several bud scales. The poplars. *Populus* spp. *Go to page 102.*
2. Winter buds with a single bud scale. The Willows. *Salix* spp. *Go to page 106.*

1. Leaf stalks long and distinctly flattened in cross section. *Go to page 102.*
2. Leaf stalks rounded or nearly so in cross section, somewhat grooved on the lower surface. *Go to page 103.*

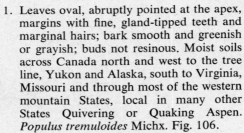

1. Leaves oval, abruptly pointed at the apex, margins with fine, gland-tipped teeth and marginal hairs; bark smooth and greenish or grayish; buds not resinous. Moist soils across Canada north and west to the tree line, Yukon and Alaska, south to Virginia, Missouri and through most of the western mountain States, local in many other States Quivering or Quaking Aspen. *Populus tremuloides* Michx. Fig. 106.
2. Leaves coarsely toothed. *Go to the next key.*

1. Leaf blades oval, rather leathery in texture, broadest slightly below the middle, rounded or slightly contracted at the base, apex not elongated, teeth somewhat pointed; buds pubescent and not resinous; bark smooth, greenish to grayish. Moist or dry soils from Nova Scotia to Manitoba, south to Virginia and Missouri. Large-toothed Aspen. *Populus grandidentata* Michx. Fig. 107.
2. Leaves broadest at the base, base straight (truncate) or slightly heart-shaped; buds resinous. *Go to the next key.*

1. Marginal teeth rounded and without callouses, blades with a distinct translucent and somewhat leathery margin, base of the blade often with 2 or more glands, apex

abruptly long, slender-pointed; only the younger parts of the trees with green or grayish, smooth bark. Manitoba to Alberta, south to Texas. Great Plains Cottonwood, Sargent Cottonwood. *Populus sargentii*. Dode. (*P. deltoides* var. *occidentalis* Rydb.). Fig. 108.

2. Marginal teeth pointed toward the leaf apex, callous-tipped, blades with translucent and somewhat leathery margins, base with 2 or more glands, truncate or slightly heart-shaped, apex not abruptly pointed; old bark gray and deeply ridged, young bark smooth and greenish; buds resinous. Southern Quebec to Ontario and probably Manitoba south to Florida and Texas. Southern Cottonwood. *Populus deltoides* Marsh. Fig. 109.

Some botanists consider the Great Plains Cottonwood, *P. sargentii* to be variety *occidentalis* of *P. deltoides*, and the Southern Cottonwood to be *P. deltoides* var. *deltoides*.

1. Leaves narrowly long-elliptical or lance-like gradually tapering to each end, 3 or more times as long as broad, petioles short, margins with fine teeth terminating in callouses; young twigs light gray and smooth, older branches and trunks with very rough bark; bud scales resinous. Banks of streams in southwestern Saskatchewan and southern Alberta, south to New Mexico and California. Narrow-leaf Cottonwood. *Populus angustifolia* James. Fig. 110.

2. Leaves broader and not more than 3 times as long as broad, rounded at the base. *Go to the next key*.

1. Leaves green on both surfaces, slightly lighter in colour on the under surface, tapering from well below the middle to the

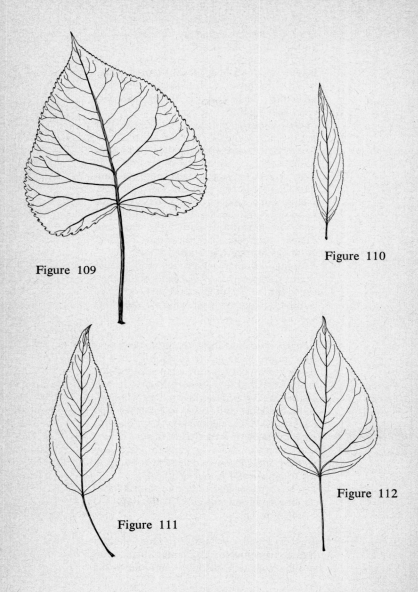

Figure 109

Figure 110

Figure 111

Figure 112

narrow, pointed apex, base rounded, upper surface not resinous; bark of trunks rough, that of the younger twigs gray and smooth. Banks of streams in southern Alberta, south to Nebraska, New Mexico and Arizona. Lance-leaved Cottonwood. Smooth-bark Cottonwood. Pointed-leaf Cottonwood. *Populus acuminata* Rydb Fig. 111.

Hitchcock *et al* point out that this species occurs only where the range of *P. sargentii* and *P. angustifolia* or *P. fremontii* overlap, and may, therefore, be a hybrid of these species.
2. Leaves brownish, rusty or very light green on the under surface, usually resinous. *Go to the next key.*

1. Lower surface of the leaves pale and with a brownish, metallic lustre and resinous, very finely toothed, base of the blade rounded or very slightly heart-shaped; only the upper part of the trees with smooth, grayish bark; buds resinous and aromatic. Widely distributed in low woods and alluvial soils from Newfoundland, Labrador and Nova Scotia, west and northwest to Alaska and British Columbia, south to Pennsylvania and North Dakota. Balsam Poplar. *Populus balsamifera* L. Fig. 112.
2. Under surface of the leaves usually silvery or very light green, base of the blades rounded or heart-shaped, margins finely toothed, the teeth often callous-tipped; buds and blades resinous and aromatic; bark rough except on the younger growth. Moist soils from Alaska and British Columbia, south to Montana, Idaho and California. Black Cottonwood. *Populus trichocarpa*. T. & G. Fig. 113.

Swamp Cottonwood, *Populus heterophylla* extends irregularly northward along the Atlantic Coastal Plain as far as Massachusetts and in the Mississippi River basin in Ohio, Michigan, Indiana, Illinois and southward to the Gulf of Mexico.

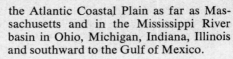

1. Leaves usually 3 or more times longer than broad. *Go to page 106.*
2. Leaves usually less than 3 times as long as broad. *Go to page 108.*

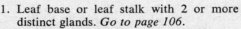

1. Leaf base or leaf stalk with 2 or more distinct glands. *Go to page 106.*
2. Leaf base or leaf stalk without glands. *Go to page 106.*

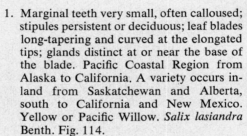

1. Marginal teeth very small, often calloused; stipules persistent or deciduous; leaf blades long-tapering and curved at the elongated tips; glands distinct at or near the base of the blade. Pacific Coastal Region from Alaska to California. A variety occurs inland from Saskatchewan and Alberta, south to California and New Mexico. Yellow or Pacific Willow. *Salix lasiandra* Benth. Fig. 114.
2. Marginal teeth distinct; upper surface of the leaves glossy or shining, blades thick and with a long, slender-pointed apex, bases tapering to the petioles; glands on the petioles distinct. Small trees or shrubs from Newfoundland to Alberta, south to Maryland and Iowa. Shining Willow. *Salix lucida* Muhl. Fig. 115.

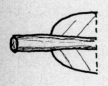

1. Stipules usually persistent at the base of the petioles; leaves long, narrow, with a long, often curved tip, green on the lower surface, lateral veins uniting to form a marginal vein; bases of the petioles continuous on the twigs (decurrent). New Brunswick, southwestern Quebec and southern Ontario, west to Minnesota and

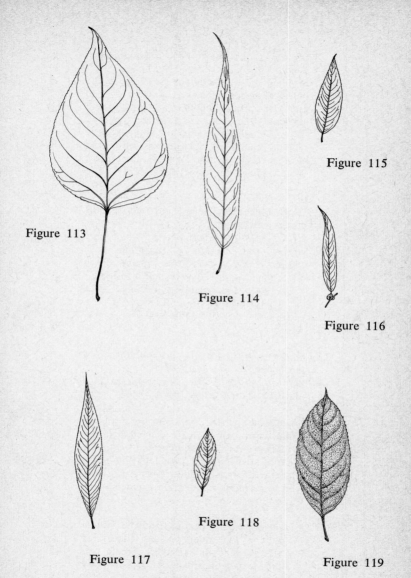

Figure 113

Figure 114

Figure 115

Figure 116

Figure 117

Figure 118

Figure 119

South Dakota, south to Florida and Texas. Black Willow. *Salix nigra* L. Fig. 116.

2. Stipules not persistent at the base of the petioles; under surface of the leaf whitish and glaucous, blades long-tipped and curved at the apex; twigs slender, yellowish and tending to droop. Southwestern Quebec to British Columbia, south and west to Kentucky and Arizona. Peach-leaf Willow. *Salix amygdaloides* Anderss. Fig. 117.

1. Leaf base or petiole with distinct glands, blades thick, apex long, slender-pointed, base narrowing to the petiole, upper surface glossy or shining, marginal teeth distinct. Small trees or shrubs from Newfoundland to Alberta, south to Maryland and Iowa. Shining Willow. *Salix lucida* Muhl. Fig. 115.

2. Leaf base or petiole without glands. *Go to the next key.*

1. Under surface of the leaf glabrous at maturity. *Go to page 108.*

2. Under surface of the leaf pubescent at maturity. *Go to page 109.*

1. Leaves 2-6 inches long, tapering to a long, curved apex, under surface whitish; twigs slender, yellowish and tending to droop. Widely distributed from Southwestern Quebec to British Columbia, south and west to Kentucky and Arizona. Peach-leaf Willow. *Salix amygdaloides* Anderss. Fig. 117.

2. Leaves elliptical tapering from the middle to both ends, under surface silvery or whitish, upper surface dark green and shining, veins on lower surface slightly raised (reticulate). Small trees or shrubs from Newfoundland and Nova Scotia to

British Columbia, south to Delaware, Kentucky, Missouri and Montana. Glaucous or Pussy Willow. *Salix discolor* Muhl. Fig. 118.

1. Under surface of the leaves silvery or bluish and with a whitish or brownish pubescence, veins rather prominent (reticulate) and the surface roughened, blades elliptical or oblong, abruptly pointed at the apex; branchlets grayish-pubescent. Small trees or shrubs across Canada and the northern States. Beak Willow, Bebb's Willow. *Salix bebbiana* Sarg. Fig. 78.
2. Under surface of the leaves densely white-pubescent, the upper surface slightly so, blade elliptical to obovate, apex abruptly pointed, margins slightly toothed; twigs densely pubescent. Pacific Coastal Region from southern British Columbia to California. Hooker's Willow. *Salix hookeriana* Barratt. Fig. 119.

LEAVES ALTERNATE AND COMPOUND

1. Leaves trifoliate and with translucent dots; fruit about 1 inch in diameter and broadly winged. Small trees or shrubs in woods and thickets. Local in Quebec, the counties along Lake Erie in Ontario, west to Nebraska, south to Florida and Texas. Common Hop Tree. *Ptelea trifoliata* L. Fig. 120.
2. Leaves not trifoliate. *Go to the next key.*

1. Leaves simple pinnate or bipinnate without a terminal leaflet (even pinnate). *Go to page 110.*
2. Leaves simple pinnate or bipinnate but with a terminal leaflet present (odd pinnate.) *Go to page 110.*

1. Trees with the trunks and branches having stout, usually branched thorns; leaflets comparatively small, not over 1 1/2 inches long and 1/2 inch wide; fruit a pod 10-18 inches long, flat, curved or twisted and dark, glossy brown. Local in Essex county, Ontario, Pennsylvania, west to Nebraska, southwest to Georgia, Louisiana and Texas. A much planted tree. Common Honey Locust. *Gleditsia triacanthos* L. Fig. 121.

2. Trees without thorns. *Go to the next key.*

1. Leaves large with several (5-9) branches (pinnae) each pinnately divided; leaflets about 2 1/2 inches long and 1 inch broad, abruptly pointed, lowest leaflet on a pinna not paired; fruit large pods about 6 inches long and 2 or more inches broad, pod walls thick and leathery; seeds large, about 3/4 inch long. New York, local in Essex County, Ontario, west to South Dakota, south to West Virginia and Oklahoma. Frequently cultivated. Kentucky Coffee Tree. *Gymnocladus dioica* (L.) K. Koch. Fig. 122.

2. Leaves simple pinnate with 10-22 leaflets, with or without the remains of a terminal leaflet; leaflets with a very short, non-glandular pubescence on the lower surface, leaflets lance-like with a long-tapering apex; fruit a globose, indehiscent nut about 2 inches in diameter and roughened but not sticky or glandular; leaf scars without a hairy fringe; pith of the twigs with cross walls. New York, southwestern Ontario, west to South Dakota, south to Florida and Texas. Black Walnut. *Juglans nigra* L. Fig. 131.

1. Trees with the stipules modified to form thorns; leaflets few to many, elliptical,

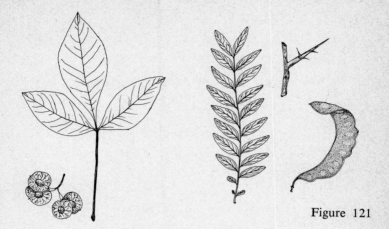

Figure 120

Figure 121

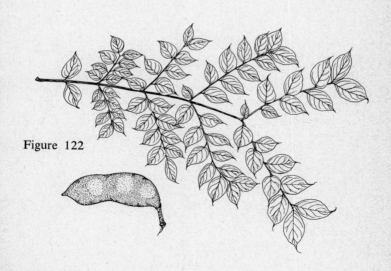

Figure 122

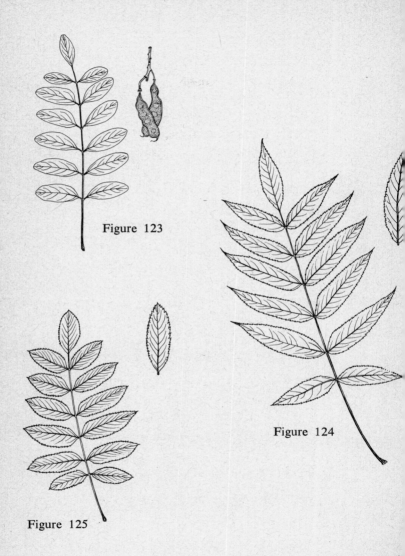

Figure 123

Figure 124

Figure 125

rounded at the apex; fruit flat, bean-like pods. Native in the Appalachian Mountains from Pennsylvania to Alabama, and in the Ozark Region. However, it is widely cultivated and now naturalized north to southern Ontario and Nova Scotia. Black or Common Locust. *Robinia pseudoacacia* L. Fig. 123.

2. Trees without thorns and the fruits not bean-like pods. *Go to the next key.*

1. Fruits resembling miniature apples; inflorescences and fruits in flat-topped or rounded clusters. Mountain Ashes. *Sorbus* spp. *Go to page 113.*

2. Fruit a nut, or berry-like and in dense clusters or racemes. *Go to page 114.*

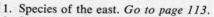

1. Species of the east. *Go to page 113.*
2. Species of the west. *Go to page 113.*

1. Leaflets 13-17, tapering from an oblique base to a slender-pointed tip, about 3-5 times longer than broad; fruits about 1/4 inch in diameter; bark smooth and grayish. Small trees or shrubs in moist or dry soils from Newfoundland to Manitoba and Minnesota, south to Georgia and Tennessee. American Mountain Ash. *Sorbus americana* Marsh. Fig. 124.

2. Leaflets 7-13, elliptical or oblong with short-pointed tips, 2-3 times as long as broad; fruit about 3/8 inch in diameter. Small trees or shrubs in moist or dry soils from Newfoundland to Manitoba and Minnesota, south to New York and Iowa. *Sorbus decora* (Sarg.) C. K. Schneid. Fig. 125.

1. Young growth with reddish or brownish hairs; leaflets oblong to long-oval, somewhat rounded at the tips or very abruptly

pointed, leaflet margins toothed for about 3/4 of their length; fruit red but with a dense whitish bloom. Alaska and Yukon to British Columbia and California, east to Montana. *Sorbus sitchensis* Roemer. Fig. 126.

2. Young growth with whitish hairs; leaflets lance-like and long-pointed; leaflet margins toothed for about their entire length; fruit orange or bright red and without whitish bloom. Alaska to British Columbia, western Alberta and the Cypress Hills, south to California and New Mexico. *Sorbus scopulina* Greene. Fig. 127.

1. Small trees or shrubs; fruits in drooping panicles or compact, upright, cone-shaped clusters. *Go to page 114.*
2. Trees producing nuts with persistent or deciduous husks. *Go to page 116.*

1. Leaflets not sharply toothed; inflorescence and fruit drooping or spreading; fruits whitish and smooth, rather ridged. Small trees or shrubs in low, wet areas or in swampy ground in southern Quebec and Ontario, Maine to Minnesota, south to Florida and Texas. Poison Sumac. *Rhus vernix* L. Fig. 128.

   Contact with this species may produce a rash and blisters similar to those caused by Poison Ivy.

2. Leaflets sharply toothed; flowers and fruits in dense, erect, cone-shaped clusters. *Go to the next key.*

1. Twigs and under surface of the leaves quite hairy; flowers and fruits in compact, cone-like clusters, individual fruits small, red, and covered wth erect or spreading acid-tasting hairs, seeds stone-like; wood orange or yellowish in colour. Dry soils

114

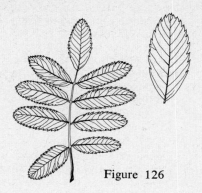

Figure 126

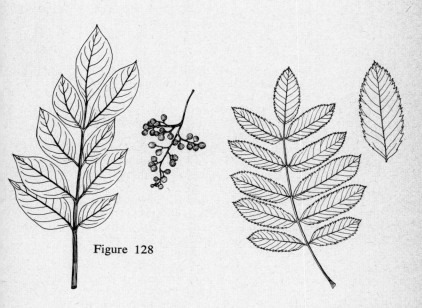

Figure 128

Figure 127

Nova Scotia to Ontario and Minnesota, south to North Carolina and Illinois. Staghorn Sumac. *Rhus typhina* L. Fig. 129.

2. Twigs and leaves without hairs (glabrous); flowers and fruits similar to the previous species but the fruits with short, appressed hairs. Southern Quebec to British Columbia, south to Florida and Texas. Smooth Sumac. *Rhus glabra* L.

1. Leaves with 11-23 leaflets; pith of the twigs chambered or with cross walls; husks of the nuts not splitting open. Walnut and Butternut. *Juglans* spp. *Go to page 116*.

2. Leaves with 5-9 leaflets; pith of the twigs not chambered or without cross walls; husks of the nuts usually splitting open; leaves and fruits usually aromatic. The Hickories. *Carya* spp. *Go to page 118*.

1. Leaves with 11-17 leaflets, leaflets lance-like, toothed, petioles and branchlets covered with sticky hairs; fruits elliptical or oblong, glandular and sticky; pith dark brown and with cross walls; upper margins of the leaf scars with a fringe of hairs. New Brunswick, southwestern Quebec and southern Ontario, west to Minnesota, south to Georgia and Arkansas. Butternut. *Juglans cinerea* L. Fig. 130.

2. Leaves with 11-23 leaflets and with a very short, non-glandular pubescence on the lower surface, terminal leaflet often reduced or absent, leaflets lance-like with a long, tapering apex; fruits globose, about 2 inches in diameter and roughened but not sticky; leaf scars without a hairy fringe. New York, southwestern Ontario, west to South Dakota, south to Florida and Texas. Black Walnut. *Juglans nigra* L. Fig. 131.

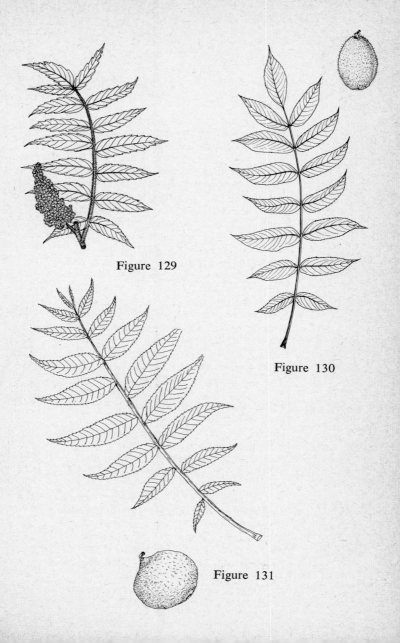

Figure 129

Figure 130

Figure 131

1. Leaves most frequently with 5 leaflets, occasionally with 7 on younger trees or branches. *Go to page 118.*
2. Leaves most frequently with 7-9 leaflets. *Go to page 118.*

1. Buds large, about 5/8 inch long and 3/8 inch broad, scales brownish or gray, abruptly contracted to an elongated, reflexed tip, outer scales hairy but not glandular, inner scales with resinous glands; bark loosening into thick sheets free at the upper and lower ends; marginal teeth with a tuft of hairs just above or below their apices, terminal leaflet the largest; husks of the nuts thick, shell thin, kernel sweet and edible. Southwestern Quebec to Wisconsin and Nebraska, south to Georgia and Texas. Shagbark Hickory. *Carya ovata* (Mill.) K. Koch. Fig. 132.
2. Winter buds sharp-pointed, about 3/8 inch long, outer scales deciduous, inner scales pubescent and glandular; bark coarsely ridged and furrowed; husks thin, shell thin, kernel slightly bitter tasting. Irregularly distributed in southern Ontario, New England to Michigan, Illinois and Kansas, south to Florida and Texas. Pignut Hickory. *Carya glabra* (Mill.) Sweet. Fig. 133.

1. Under surface of the leaflets with a soft, velvety pubescence. *Go to page 118.*
2. Under surface of the leaflets without a pubescence or almost so. *Go to page 122.*

1. Winter buds about 5/8 inch long, scales pubescent and glandular; fruit 2-3 inches long and with a thick husk and shell; leaflets most frequently 7, soft pubescent on the lower surface; twigs slightly pubescent and brownish. Rare in the Niagara Peninsula and extreme southwestern Ontario

118

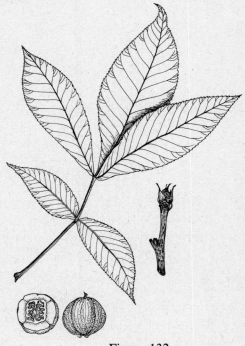

Figure 132

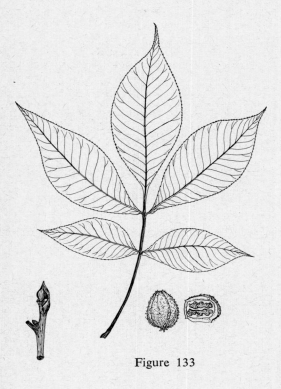

Figure 133

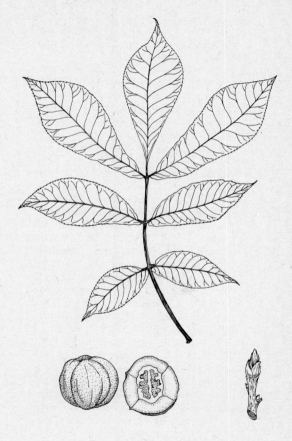

Figure 134

and Michigan, scattered in New York and other eastern States and southward to Georgia. It is most frequent in the upper parts of the Mississippi and Ohio River Basins west to Iowa and Oklahoma. Kingnut, Shellbark Hickory. *Carya laciniosa* (Michx. f.) Loud. Fig. 134.

2. Winter buds about 3/4 inch long, bud scales reddish-brown, outer scales deciduous and exposing the inner silky scales; leaves resinous dotted; branchlets pubescent; husks of the fruit thick, nut shell thick. Extremely rare or extinct in southern Ontario, New England, west to Iowa, south to Florida and Texas. Mockernut Hickory. *Carya tomentosa* (Poir.) Nutt.

1. Winter buds slender, scales paired and densely covered with sulphur-yellow, resinous dots; husks of the fruit thin, shell thin, kernel not palatable; bark tight on the trunks; leaflets with some pubescence on the under surface but not velvet-like. Upland woods in southwestern Quebec and southern Ontario, New England, west to Minnesota, south to Florida and Texas. Bitternut Hickory. *Carya cordiformis* (Wang.) K. Koch. Fig. 135.

2. Winter buds stout, not sharp pointed, 1/4-3/8 inch long, scales pubescent and somewhat glandular; bark rough and scaly but not breaking into sheets; husk thin, shell thin, kernel edible. Massachusetts, west to Ontario and Wisconsin, south to Georgia and Arkansas. Red Hickory, Sweet Pignut Hickory. *Carya ovalis* (Wang.) Sarg. Fig. 136.

Pecan, *Carya illinoensis* of the Mississippi River valley, extends northward into Indiana, Illinois and Kansas.

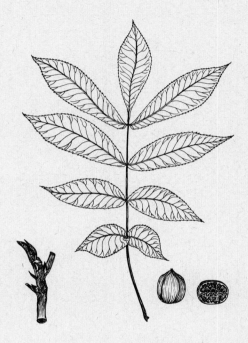

Figure 135

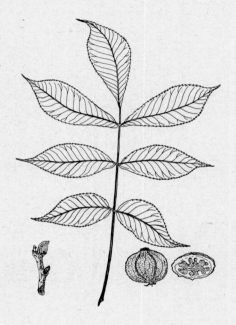

Figure 136

Summary of Leaf
and Fruit Characteristics

EVERGREENS

Leaves scale-like and branchlets flattened. The Cedars, *page 23*.

Leaves scale- or awl-like and branchlets rounded or angular. The Junipers, *page 25*.

Leaves clustered on short branches and deciduous. The Larches, *page 26*.

Leaves in fascicles of 21-5. The Pines, *page 35*.

Leaves in fascicles of 5, Limber Pine, Western White Pine, White Pine, Whitebark Pine, *page 35*.

Leaves in fascicles of 3. Pitch Pine, Ponderosa Pine, *page 37*.

Leaves in fascicles of 2, Jack Pine, Lodgepole Pine, Red Pine, *page 38*.

Leaves with stalked bases, Douglas Fir, *page 33*; Hemlocks, *page 31*; Yews, *page 29*.

Leaves not stalked. Balsams or Firs, *page 33*; Spruces, *page 29*.

Leaves with decurrent bases. Hemlocks, *page 31*; Spruces, *page 29*; Yews, *page 29*.

EVERGREEN FRUITS

Fruit a red stone fruit. Yews, *page 29*.

Fruit a bluish stone fruit. Junipers, *page 25*.

Cones globular, scales few and with sharp dorsal prickles. Yellow Cedar, *page 23*.

Cones with few, opposite, flexible scales. Cedars, *page 23*.

Cones with 3-pronged bracts protruding from under the scales. Douglas Fir, *page 33*.

Cones with a simple bract protruding from under the scales. Larches, *page 26*.

Cones erect. Balsams or Firs, *page 33*.

Cone scales deciduous. Balsams or Firs, *page 33*.

THE BROAD-LEAVED TREES

LEAVES OPPOSITE

Leaves simple. Dogwoods, *page 42*; Maples, *page 45*; Viburnums, *page 42*; Wahoo, *page 43*.

Leaves compound. Ashes, *page 53*; Elders, *page 51*; Manitoba Maple, *page 51*.

Leaves simple – margins not toothed. Dogwoods, page 42; Viburnums, *page 42*.

Leaves simple – margins toothed or palmately lobed. Maples, *page 45*; Viburnums, *page 42*; Wahoo, *page 43*.

FRUITS

Fruit berry-like. Elders (blue, black or red), *page 51*; Wahoo (reddish or purplish), *page 43*.

Fruit with a central stone or pit. Dogwoods (red), *page 42*; Viburnums (blue, *page 42*.

Fruits winged (samaras). Ashes (wing terminal), *page 53*; Maples (fruits paired), *page 45*.

Fruits splitting open when mature. Wahoo (reddish or purplish), *page 43*.

LEAVES ALTERNATE AND LEAVES SIMPLE

Alders, *page 81*; Alternate-leaved Dogwood, *page 75*; Arbutus, *page 74*; Basswood, *page 83*; Beech, *page 86*; Birches, *page 92*, Blue Beech, *page 89*; Cascara, *page 75*; Cherries, *page 99*; Chestnut, *page 86*; Cottonwoods, *page 102*; Crab Apples, *page 59*; Elms, *page 84*; Hackberry, *page 83*; Hawthorn, *page 59*; Ironwood, *page 89*; June-berry, *page 97*; Magnolia, *page 72*; Mulberry, *page 57*; Oaks, *page 60*; Pawpaw, *page 72*; Plums, *page 98*; Poplars, *page 102*; Redbud, *page 74*; Sassafras, *page 60*; Sour Gum, *page 71*; Sycamore, *page 57*; Tulip Tree, *page 60*; Willows, *pages 77, 106*; Witch Hazel, *page 79*.

All or some of the leaves not lobed or toothed (margins entire). Alternate-leaved Dogwood, *page 75*; Arbutus, *page 74*; Cascara, *page 75*; Magnolia, *page 72*; Pawpaw, *page 72*; Redbud, *page 74*; Sassafras, *page 60*; Sour Gum, *page 71*; Willows, *page 77*;

Leaf margins lobed. Alders, *page 81*; Crab Apples, *page 59*; Hawthorns, *page 59*; Mulberry, *page 57*; Oaks, *page 60*; Sassafras, *page 60*; Sour Gum, *page 71*; Sycamore, *page 57*; Tulip Tree, *page 60*.

Leaf margins wavy, undulate, sinuate or very shallowly lobed. Alders, *page 81*; Oak spp., *page 79*; Witch Hazel, *page 79*.

Leaf margins with simple teeth. Basswood, *page 83*; Beech, *page 86*; Birch spp. *page 88*; Blue Beech, *page 89*; Cascara, *page 88*; Cherries, *page 99*; Chestnut, *page 86*; Cottonwoods, *page 102*; Crab Apples, *page 70*; Hackberry, *page 83*; Hawthorns, *page 70*; Ironwood, *page 89*; June-berry, *page 97*; Mulberry, *page 96*; Oak spp. *page 79*; Plums, *page 98*; Poplars, *page 102*; Willows, *page 106*.

Leaf margins double-toothed. Alders, *page 91*; Birch spp., *page 92*; Blue Beech, *page 95*; Crab Apples, *page 98*; Elms, *page 84*; Hawthorns, *page 97*; Ironwood, *page 95*; Plums, *page 98*.

Leaves with the bases of the petioles hollow and covering the buds. Sycamore, *page 57*; Tulip Tree, *page 60*.

Nearly all of the main veins of the leaf readily traceable to the leaf margins. Alders, *pages 81, 91*; Beech, *page 86*; Birch spp., *page 92*; Blue Beech, *page 95*; Chestnut, *page 86*; Crab Apples, *page 70*; Elms, *page 84*; Hawthorns, *page 70*; Ironwood, *page 89*; Oak spp., *page 60*; Sycamore, *page 57*.

FRUITS

Fruits berry-like. Arbutus (red), *page 74*; Cascara (blue or black), *page 75*; Mulberry (red), *page 57*.

Fruits with a central stone or pit. Alternate-leaved Dogwood (blue), *page 75*; Cherries (red), *page 99*; Hackberry (reddish or purplish), *page 83*; Plums (red), *page 98*; Sassafras (blue), *page 60*; Sour Gum (blue), *page 71*.

Fruits splitting open when mature. Cottonwoods, (small capsules), *page 102*; Magnolia (large, fleshy, reddish), *page 72*; Poplars (small capsules), *page 102*; Willows (small capsules), *pages 77, 106*; Witch Hazel (woody capsules), *page 79*.

Fruit a nut. Basswood (attached to a wing), *page 83*; Beech (bur-like), *page 86*; Chestnut (large, bur-like or spiny), *page 86*; Oaks (acorns), *page 60*.

Fruits winged. Alders (small, marginally winged, sometimes mere ridges or absent), *pages 81, 91*; Basswood (wing free from the nut). *page 83*; Birches (small and 2-winged), *page 92*; Blue Beech (wing large and 3-lobed), *page 89*; Elm (wing marginal) *page 84*; Tulip Tree (fruit in a cone), *page 60*.

Fruit a globular ball of small nutlets. Sycamore, *page 57*.

Fruit like miniature apples. Crab Apples, *page 59*; Hawthorns (seeds hard nutlets) *pages 59*; June-berry (reddish or purplish), *page 97*.

Fruit large and fleshy. Magnolia (red and somewhat cone-like), *page 72*; Pawpaw (seeds very large), *page 72*.

Fruit bladderlike. Ironwood (arranged in catkins), *page 89*.

Fruits cone-like. Magnolia (red and somewhat fleshy), *page 72*; Tulip Tree, *page 60*.

LEAVES ALTERNATE AND COMPOUND

Leaves trifoliate. Hop Tree, *page 109*.

Leaves simple pinnate. Black Locust, *page 110*. Butternut, *page 116*; Hickories, *page 118*; Mountain Ashes, *page 113*; Sumacs, *page 114*; Walnut, *page 116*;

Leaves bi- or tripinnate. Honey locust, *page 110*; Kentucky Coffee Tree, *page 110*.

Leaves or leaf branches even pinnate. Honey Locust, *page 110*; Kentucky Coffee Tree, *page 110*; Walnut, *page 110*.

Leaves odd pinnate. Black Locust, *page 110*; Butternut, *page 116*; Hickories, *page 118*; Mountain Ashes, *page 113*; Sumacs, *page 114*; Walnut, *page 116*.

FRUITS

Fruit berry-like or a small stone fruit. Sumacs (red and hairy, or greenish and smooth), *page 114*.

Fruit a nut. Butternut (large and sticky), *page 116*; Hickories (husk usually splitting into 4 valves), *page 118*; Walnut (large, round and not sticky), *page 116*.

Fruit winged. Hop Tree, *page 109*.

Fruit like miniature apples. Mountain Ashes (red or orange-coloured), *page 113*.

Fruits bean-like pods. Black Locust (pods flat and thin), *page 110*; Honey Locust (pods long, thin and twisted), *page 110*; Kentucky Coffee Tree (pods large, covering thick and fleshy), *page 110*.

GLOSSARY

APPRESSED.   Lying against the supporting organ.

ASYMMETRICAL.   When one side of a leaf or other structure is not equal to the other side, e.g. Elm or Basswood leaf.

AXIL.   The angle between the petiole of a leaf and the stem.

AXILLARY.   Refers to the position of flowers, buds etc., when they are in the axils of the leaves.

BERRY.   A fleshy fruit in which the two to many seeds are embedded in a central fleshy tissue, e.g. Tomato.

BLADE.   The broad expanded part of the leaf.

BLOOM.   A whitish coating covering the surface of certain plants or parts of plants.

BRACT.   A reduced leaf or a modified leaf subtending certain plant structures.

CALLOUS.   A hardened point or glandular structure at the tip of a tooth or lobe of a leaf.

CAPSULE.   A dry fruit formed from two or more united ovaries or carpels, and when mature, splitting into as many divisions as there are carpels.

CARPEL.   The unit part of the ovary. It may be simple or compound and united.

CATKIN.   A name applied to reduced flowers occurring in a close raceme, e.g. Willows and Birches.

COMPOUND LEAF.   A leaf divided into two or more leaflets; leaflets are characterized by the lack of buds in their axils.

CORYMB.   A branching type of inflorescence in which the lower flower stalks are longer than the central short stalks; this produces a flat-topped inflorescence.

CYME.   A branching raceme type of inflorescence.

DECIDUOUS.   The falling off of any part of the plant, e.g. the leaves in the fall.

DECURRENT.   When the base of a leaf petiole or a branch continues a distance down the stem, it is said to be decurrent.

DIOECIOUS.   Male and female flowers on different plants.

DOUBLE-SERRATE.   The presence of a large tooth followed by one or more smaller teeth.

DRUPE.   A fruit similar to a cherry or plum with a stony pit surrounded by a fleshy covering.

ENTIRE.   When a leaf margin of lobe has no teeth or divisions.
EROSE.   Appearing ragged or as if chewed or gnawed.

FASCICLE.   A bundle or cluster closely associated at the base.

GLABROUS.   Smooth and without pubescence.
GLAUCOUS.   Covered with a whitish coating or bloom.

INFLORESCENCE.   The arrangement of flowers on a flowering plant, and subsequently the arrangement of the fruits.

LEAFLET.   A single unit of a compound leaf.
LEAF SCAR.   The scar left on a twig when the leaf drops.
LEGUME.   The pod-like fruit produced by most members of the Legume family, e.g. Peas and Beans.

OBOVATE.   Inversely egg-shaped, i.e. broadest at the apex.
OVAL.   Broadly elliptical; flattened at the sides and rounded at the apex and base (like a race track, arena or stadium).
OVATE.   Egg-shaped, i.e. broadest at the base.

PALMATE.   A branching of veins, or a leaf form suggesting the radiating of the fingers from the palm of the hand, e.g., the Maples.
PANICLE.   A branching inflorescence with numerous secondary branches and the flowers usually all at the same stage of development.
PETIOLE.   The stalk of a leaf.
PINNATE.   (Feather-like). Veins or leaflets arising from a central vein or axis.
PUBESCENT.   Covered with hairs.

RACEME.   An inflorescence where the stalked flowers arise alternately from a common stalk or rachis.
RACHIS.   A common stem or axis from which leaves, leaflets or flowers may arise.
REFLEXED.   Turned backward, often rather abruptly.
RETICULATE.   Veins prominent and forming a network.
REVOLUTE.   The turning or rolling of the margins of the leaves or leaflets toward the under surface.

SAMARA.   A winged fruit as in the Maple or Ash.
SERRATE.   Sharply toothed.

SESSILE. Without a stalk.

SHRUB. Usually distinguished from a tree by its smaller stature and the tendency to grow several stems from a common root.

SIMPLE. A leaf that is complete in one part as opposed to compound.

SINUS. The space or area between two lobes as in the Maple or Oak.

SPIRAL. Arranged alternately around the axis.

STALK. A general term used to designate the supporting structure of any part of a plant, e.g. the petiole of the leaf, the peduncle or pedicel of a flower or fruit.

STIPULE. A little leaf- or scale-like bract that occurs on the stem or branch on each side of the leaf base where it joins the stem. It does not occur on all plants.

STOMA. (Pl. Stomata). The minute, invisible pores scattered on the surface of leaves or stems. In the evergreens these are usually arranged in lines and, therefore, their position is readily seen.

TRUNCATE. When a leaf tip or base appears as if cut off, e.g. the apex of the leaf of the Tulip tree.

UMBEL. An inflorescence in which the stalks of the flowers originate at the apex of the stem or branch.

UMBELLATE. Having the appearance of an umbel.

WHORL. The arrangement of leaves or other organs in a circle around an axis.

BIBLIOGRAPHY

BEARNS, E. R.: *Native Trees of Newfoundland and Labrador.* Department of Mines, Agriculture and Resources, St. John's, Newfoundland, 1968.

BUDD, A. C. and BEST, K. F.: *Wild Plants of the Canadian Prairies.* Queen's Printer, Ottawa, Ont., 1964.

Canada Department of Resources and Development, Forestry Branch: Native Trees of Canada. Bulletin 61. Queen's Printer, Ottawa, Ont., 1950.

DEAM, C.C.: *Flora of Indiana.* Department of Conservation, Division of Forestry, Indianapolis, Ind., 1940.

ERSKINE, D. S.: *The Plants of Prince Edward Island.* Publication 1088. Plant Research Institute, Canada Department of Agriculture, Ottawa, Ont., 1960.

FERNALD, M. L.: *Gray's Manual of Botany.* 8th Edition, American Book Company, New York, 1950.

FOX, W. S. and SOPER, J. H.: *The Distribution of some Trees and Shrubs of the Carolinian Zone of Southern Ontario.* Transactions of the Royal Canadian Institute. Part I, Vol. XXIX Part II pages 65-84, 1952; Part II, Vol. XXX Part I pages 3-32, 1953; Part III, Vol. XXX Part II pages 99-130, 1954.

FRASER, W. P. and RUSSELL, R. C.: *A Revised Annotated List of the Plants of Saskatchewan.* University of Saskatchewan, Saskatoon, Sask., 1944.

GARMAN, E. H.: *Pocket Guide to the Trees and Shrubs of British Columbia.* Department of Lands and Forests and Water Resources, British Columbia Forest Service, B.C. Forest Service Publication B. 28. Victoria, B.C., 1963.

GLEASON, H. A.: *The New Britton and Brown Illustrated Flora of the Northeastern United States and Adjacent Canada.* Lancaster Press, Lancaster, Pennsylvania, 1952.

GLEASON, H. A. and CRONQUIST, A.: *Manual of Vascular Plants of Northeastern United States and Adjacent Canada.* D. Van Nostrand Company Incorporated, Princeton, New Jersey, 1963.

HITCHCOCK, C. L., CRONQUIST, A., OWNBEY, M. and THOMPSON, J.W.: *Vascular Plants of the Pacific Northwest,* Parts 1, 2, 3, 4, 5. University of Washington Press, Seattle, Washington, 1969.

HOSIE, R. C.: *Native Trees of Canada.* 7th Edition, Queen's Printer for Canada, Ottawa, Ont., 1969.

LAKELA, OLGA: *A flora of Northeastern Minnesota.* University of Minnesota Press, Minneapolis, Minn., 1965.

LYONS, C. P.: *Trees, Shrubs and Flowers to Know in British Columbia.* J. M. Dent & Sons, Toronto, Ont., 1962.

MARIE-VICTORIN, FRÈRE.: *Flore Laurentienne.* 2nd Edition, Les Presses de L'Université de Montréal, Montréal, Quebec, 1964.

MOSS, E. H.: *Flora of Alberta.* University of Toronto Press, Toronto, Ont., 1959.

OLMSTED, F. L., COVILLE, F. V. and KELSEY, H. P.: *Standardized Plant Names.* American Joint Committee on Horticultural Nomenclature, Salem, Mass., 1924.

PORSILD, A. E., and CODY, W. J.: *Checklist of the Vascular Plants of Continental Northwest Territories, Canada.* Plant Research Institute, Canada Department of Agriculture, Ottawa, Ont., 1968.

ROLAND, A. E. and SMITH, E. C.: The Flora of Nova Scotia. Proceedings of the Nova Scotian Institute of Science 26, part 2, 1963-64; 26, part 4, 1969, Halifax, N.S.

ROULEAU, E.: *A Checklist of the Vascular Plants of the Province of Newfoundland.* Institut Botanique de L'Université of Montréal, Montréal, Quebec. 1965.

RYDBERG, P.A.: *Flora of the Prairies and Plains of Central North America.* New York Botanical garden, New York, 1932.

SARGENT, CHARLES SPRAGUE.: *Manual of the Trees of North America.* 2nd Edition, Dover Publications, Incorporated, New York, 1922.

SCOGGAN, H. J.: *The Flora of Bic and the Gaspé Peninsula, Quebec.* Bulletin 115, National Museum of Canada, Ottawa, Ont., 1950.

SCOGGAN, H. J.: *Flora of Manitoba.* Bulletin 140, National Museum of Canada, Ottawa, Ont., 1957.

Silvics of Forest Trees of the United States. Agriculture Handbook No. 271. U.S. Department of Agriculture, Forest Service, Washington, D.C., 1965.

SOPER, J. H.: *Some Families of Restricted Range in the Carolinian Flora of Canada.* Transactions of the Royal Canadian Institute, Vol. XXXI part I, pages 69-90, 1955.

WHITE, J. H. and HOSIE, R. C.: *The Forest Trees of Ontario.* Department of Lands and Forests, Ontario, Parliament Buildings, Toronto, Ont., 1957.

INDEX

141